Life Skills for Special Needs

Personal Hygiene

by JoAnn Smith

Cover Design by
Terri Moll

Inside Illustrations
by Marty Bucella

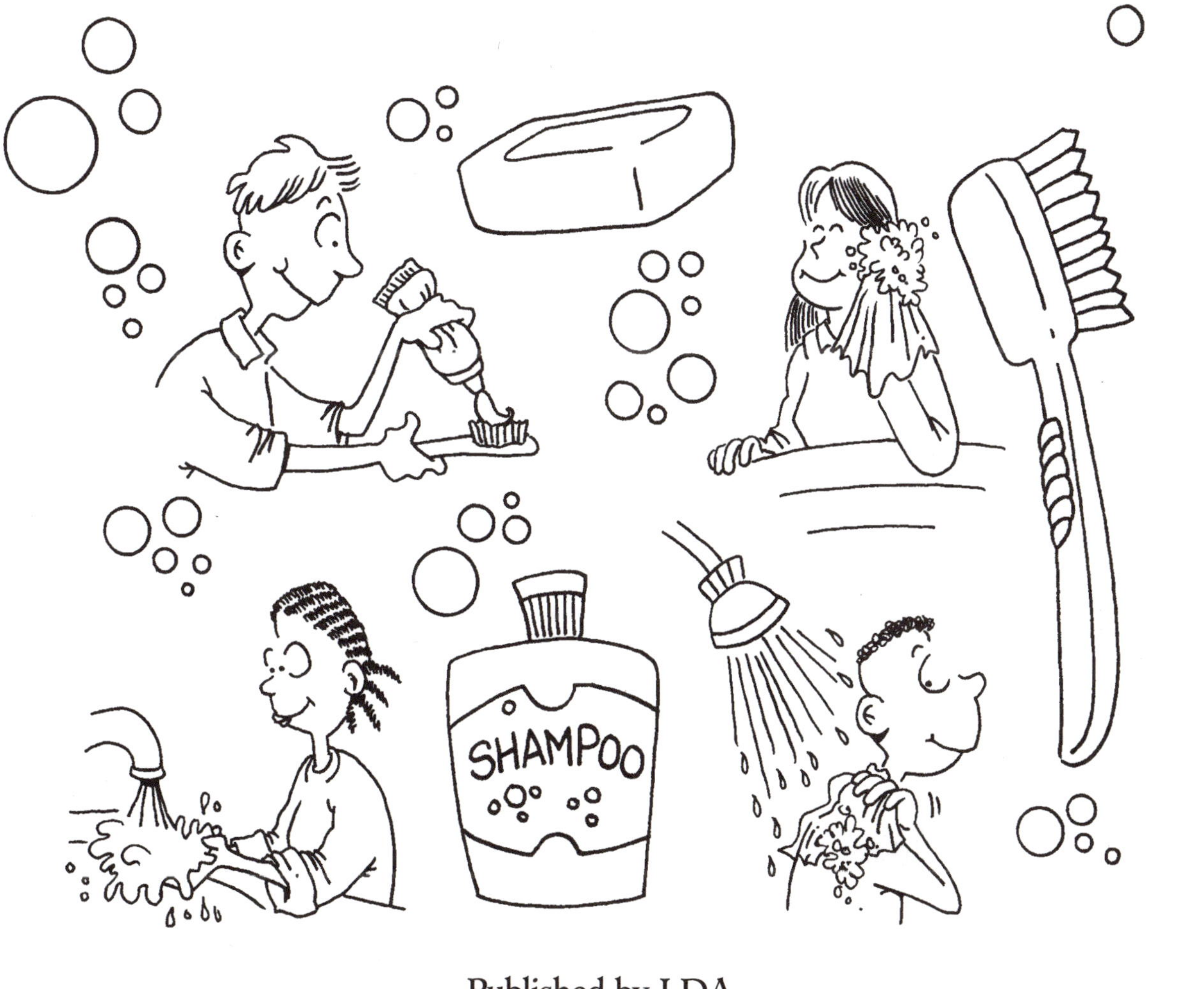

Published by LDA
an imprint of

About the Author

JoAnn C. Smith is currently a licensed professional counselor and licensed marriage and family therapist. Before she became a counselor, she taught second and third grade for five years in an inner city school. During that time, she was elected "Teacher of the Year" out of a staff of 70+ teachers. In addition to her work as an educator, she supervised a basic living skills program for chronically mentally ill adults with the Department of Mental Health and was instrumental in creating an education program that was utilized as a training center nationally. She was recognized as "Employee of the Year" at that center which employed 100+ people. She currently works extensively with severely abused children and adults.

Credits
Author: JoAnn Smith
Cover Art: Terri Moll
Inside Illustrations: Marty Bucella
Project Director: Debra Olson Pressnall
Cover Art Direction: Terri Moll
Editors: Debra Olson Pressnall and Karen Seberg
Page Design and Icon Art: Mark Conrad
Cover Photograph: ©Digital Stock

Acknowledgments
Many thanks to Frankie who encouraged me to write this book, Resa for your support and encouragement, and Pat for your creativity

Dedication
To all teachers who work with people with special needs and these special people who delight, amaze, and challenge us

McGraw-Hill Children's Publishing
A Division of The McGraw·Hill Companies

Copyright ©2001 McGraw-Hill Children's Publishing

All rights reserved. McGraw-Hill Children's Publishing grants the right to the individual purchaser to reproduce the student activity materials in this book for noncommercial individual or classroom use only. Reproduction for an entire school or school system is strictly prohibited. No part of this publication may be reproduced for storage in a retrieval system or transmitted in any form or by any means, electronic, mechanical, recording, or otherwise, without the prior written permission of the publisher. For information regarding permissions, write to McGraw-Hill Children's Publishing, P.O. Box 1650, Grand Rapids, MI 49501.

Send all other inquiries to:
McGraw-Hill Children's Publishing
3195 Wilson Drive NW
Grand Rapids, Michigan 49544

Printed in the United States of America

Personal Hygiene
ISBN: 0-7424-0200-2

1 2 3 4 5 6 7 8 9 05 04 03 02 01

Table of Contents

To the Teacher.................4

Using Toilet Tissue
    Lesson 1....................5
    Lesson 2....................7
    Lesson 3....................9

Caring for Your Teeth
    Lesson 1..................13
    Lesson 2..................15
    Lesson 3 17
    Lesson 4..................26

Washing Your Hands
    Lesson 1..................33
    Lesson 2..................35
    Lesson 3..................44

Washing Your Face
    Lesson 1 47
    Lesson 2 50
    Lesson 3..................52

Bathing
    Lesson 1..................63
    Lesson 2 67
    Lesson 3 70

Using Deodorant............80

Washing Your Hair
    Lesson 1..................83
    Lesson 2 85

Award Certificate 96

To the Teacher

The exercises in this book have been conducted with many different ages of students having special needs and various ability levels. Some of the activities address sensitive topics which are very basic to self-care. There are two important elements about which you may need to be aware if you are interested in offering successful lessons on personal hygiene. One is your attitude. If you have a matter-of-fact, "this is important basic information" attitude, your students will model your behavior. If it is a serious time, be serious, but do not hesitate at other times to be silly and have fun. The second most important element is your relationships with and knowledge of your students. If they trust you, they will do about anything you suggest, whether it seems silly or useless or hard or boring. You know what will work best for them. If appropriate, modify a lesson, improvise with easy-to-obtain equipment, divide a lesson into several stages, or whatever else will help your students master basic hygiene skills. Hopefully, these activities will provide a starting point for you to expand upon and learn with your students.

Additionally, please remember that it takes at least 30 exposures to new information for the skill to be learned. Therefore, do not hesitate to use repetition when practicing the skills. Movement and music also increase learning. It is important to utilize as many senses and mediums as possible to help students retain what they have learned.

Finally, use your community resources. You may consider contacting local merchants for possible donations of either money or supplies. In fact, they often have a certain budget for special community needs. You may also consider contacting regional offices for youth group organizations which are eager to help when informed about these needs. The American Dental Association often donates supplies for dental care. If possible, contact a local college, technical school, or cosmetology school to find out if instructors (or students) are willing to be guest speakers or provide services to your students for free or a small fee. Most people are interested in helping if they are aware of the exact need and how their volunteer services will be for a good cause. Be sure that your class or group writes thank-you letters (another important social skill activity). Not only is this good practice for your students, but the letters will also encourage future help from people in your community.

Lesson 1

Using Toilet Tissue

Objective: Student will be able to utilize an appropriate amount of toilet tissue.

Explanation: Often students will use too much or not enough toilet tissue, or will not use it at all. This activity is designed to help students learn about the appropriate amount of toilet tissue that is needed when toileting.

Materials Needed:
- Several rolls of toilet tissue

Directions to Teacher:

1.) Pass a roll of toilet tissue around the classroom so that the students can take only the amount of tissue they think they will need. (This is an open-ended activity.)

2.) When each student has taken at least one sheet of toilet tissue, announce to the class that each person has to tell one fact about him/herself for each sheet of toilet tissue removed from the roll. Examples include name, age, favorite color, number of siblings, or parents. Assist students who cannot think of enough facts by asking them questions.

3.) When this activity is completed, explain to the students that various amounts of toilet tissue fit different situations.

4.) Talk about the appropriate amount of tissue needed for urination (2–4 sheets) and bowel movements (4–5 sheets). Utilize the slang the students use for these bodily functions (examples: pee or #1; poop or #2).

5.) Have each student practice rolling out the correct amount of tissue for each bodily function.

© McGraw-Hill Children's Publishing

LL80006 *Personal Hygiene*

Name _____

Using Toilet Tissue–Lesson 1

Stick 'Em Up!

Tear off and glue the correct number of toilet tissue sheets needed for each bodily function.

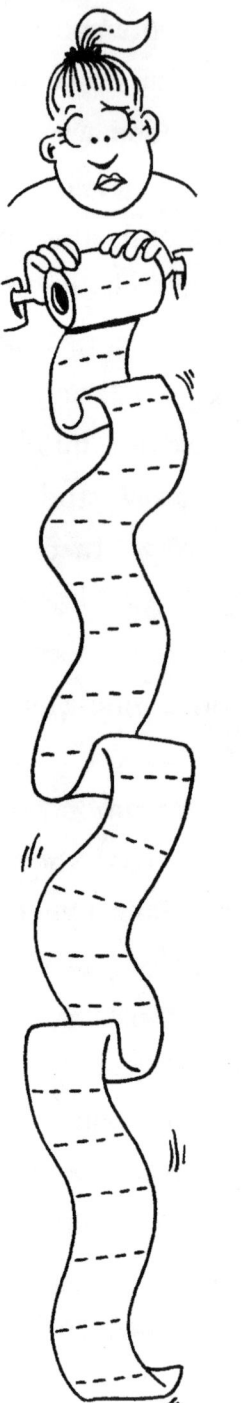

1
(urination)

2
(bowel movement)

© McGraw-Hill Children's Publishing   LL80006 *Personal Hygiene*

Lesson 2

Using Toilet Tissue

Objective: Student will be able to wipe self in an appropriate way after toileting.

Explanation: Often students wipe themselves in a way that spreads bodily wastes and encourages infections. This activity is designed to teach students how to clean themselves and maintain good hygiene.

Materials Needed:
- Rolls of toilet tissue in several different colors and fragrances
- Dolls (anatomically correct if possible)

Directions to Teacher:

Suggestion: You may have to separate the boys and girls for this activity. If that is inconvenient, make sure you, as the teacher, use a very matter-of-fact, calm voice. Show that this is a normal bodily function and not to be embarrassed about it, and that you will not allow off-color remarks with your tone of voice and body language. The students will respond accordingly. Also, to be really graphic and make your point well, you can apply something like ointment on the doll's bottoms to show the students how to clean themselves thoroughly.

1.) Explain to the students the purpose of urination and bowel movements (to rid the body of waste or "trash"). Discuss with them the fact that just as we do not spread trash around everywhere, we also do not want to spread our body waste around everywhere. Point out to them the possibility of infection if we do not clean up trash.

2.) Using the dolls, demonstrate the correct way to wipe (emphasizing front to back) in order to be clean and sanitary. Also demonstrate how a boy needs to cleanse his penis after urinating to stay healthy and eliminate body odor.

3.) Discuss why it is necessary to wipe oneself more than once to insure that the area is clean, especially after a bowel movement. Point out that the students may need to look at their toilet tissue after wiping to make sure they are clean.

4.) Have each student practice cleaning the doll. Use different fragrances, colors, and textures of toilet tissue to keep the students interested in the activity.

5.) Provide the first person who demonstrates correctly how to clean the doll an opportunity to choose a favorite roll of toilet tissue. As others demonstrate the steps correctly, have them choose a roll.

© McGraw-Hill Children's Publishing — LL80006 *Personal Hygiene*

Name _____

Using Toilet Tissue–Lesson 2

Which Way?

Draw an arrow (→) to point from front to back on each of the characters below.

Lesson 3

Using Toilet Tissue

Objective: Student will know how to use toilet tissue properly without creating plumbing problems.

Explanation: Students often use too much toilet tissue at one time which clogs the commode and causes plumbing problems where they live.

Materials Needed:
- Flash cards (see pattern pages 10–11)
- Small-mouthed jar
- Roll of toilet tissue
- Bowl of water
- Plastic tablecloth or lots of newspaper

Advance Preparation:
Photocopy and glue the flash cards to poster board. Color them as desired.

Directions to Teacher:
1.) Spread the tablecloth or newspaper on a table.
2.) Place the jar which contains a small amount of water on top of the cloth or paper.
3.) Wet three to five sheets of toilet tissue at a time and drop them into the mouth of the jar.
4.) Repeat this step until the mouth of the jar is full.
5.) Attempt to pour the water from the bowl into the jar and demonstrate how it spills everywhere.
6.) Explain to the students that this is what happens to the commode if someone puts too much toilet tissue in it. Remind the students that the water in the commode is not clean because it has urine and/or feces in it. Emphasize how nasty and smelly it is and how it can cause disease.
7.) Discuss with the students how to prevent this from happening by flushing the toilet when they finish wiping or at least after every four wipes, even if they still need to wipe some more.
8.) Using the flash cards, play a game with students. Hold up the flash cards one number at a time, as the students count out loud. When the number 4 is shown, encourage everyone to make a flushing noise before showing the toilet card. Be sure to see who can make the best flushing sound. Do everything you can to make this a silly, fun game. This activity will help students remember to flush frequently.

© McGraw-Hill Children's Publishing

LL80006 *Personal Hygiene*

Using Toilet Tissue

Lesson 3—Flash Cards

Using Toilet Tissue

Lesson 3–Flash Cards

11

© McGraw-Hill Children's Publishing

LL80006 *Personal Hygiene*

Name _____

Using Toilet Tissue–Lesson 3

1, 2, 3, Flush!

Color in each number. Cut out and paste a toilet on each number 4.

1	2	3	4
1	2	3	4
1	2	3	4
1	2	3	4
1	2	3	4

12

© McGraw-Hill Children's Publishing

LL80006 *Personal Hygiene*

Lesson 1

Caring for Your Teeth

Objective: Student will be able to place the appropriate amount of toothpaste on a toothbrush in the correct way.

Explanation: Students often use too much or not enough toothpaste when brushing their teeth. This activity is designed to help students practice applying the correct amount of toothpaste to a toothbrush.

Materials Needed:

- Toothbrush and small tube of toothpaste for each student (Local dentists will often supply this free of charge.)
- Several tubes of uniquely flavored toothpaste
- Old newspapers

Directions to Teacher:

1.) Demonstrate how to apply the appropriate amount of toothpaste to the toothbrush.
2.) Spread a sheet of newspaper on each student's desk.
3.) Give each student a toothbrush and a tube of toothpaste. Encourage the students to practice applying the correct amount of toothpaste to their brushes.
4.) When the students have completed this step successfully several times, reward them by offering them an opportunity to taste the unusually flavored toothpastes.
5.) Encourage each student to use a favorite flavor to brush his/her teeth.

Name _____

Caring for Your Teeth—Lesson 1

Pretty Brushes

Use your marker or crayon to color each toothbrush the correct color. Then draw the toothpaste on each toothbrush using that same color.

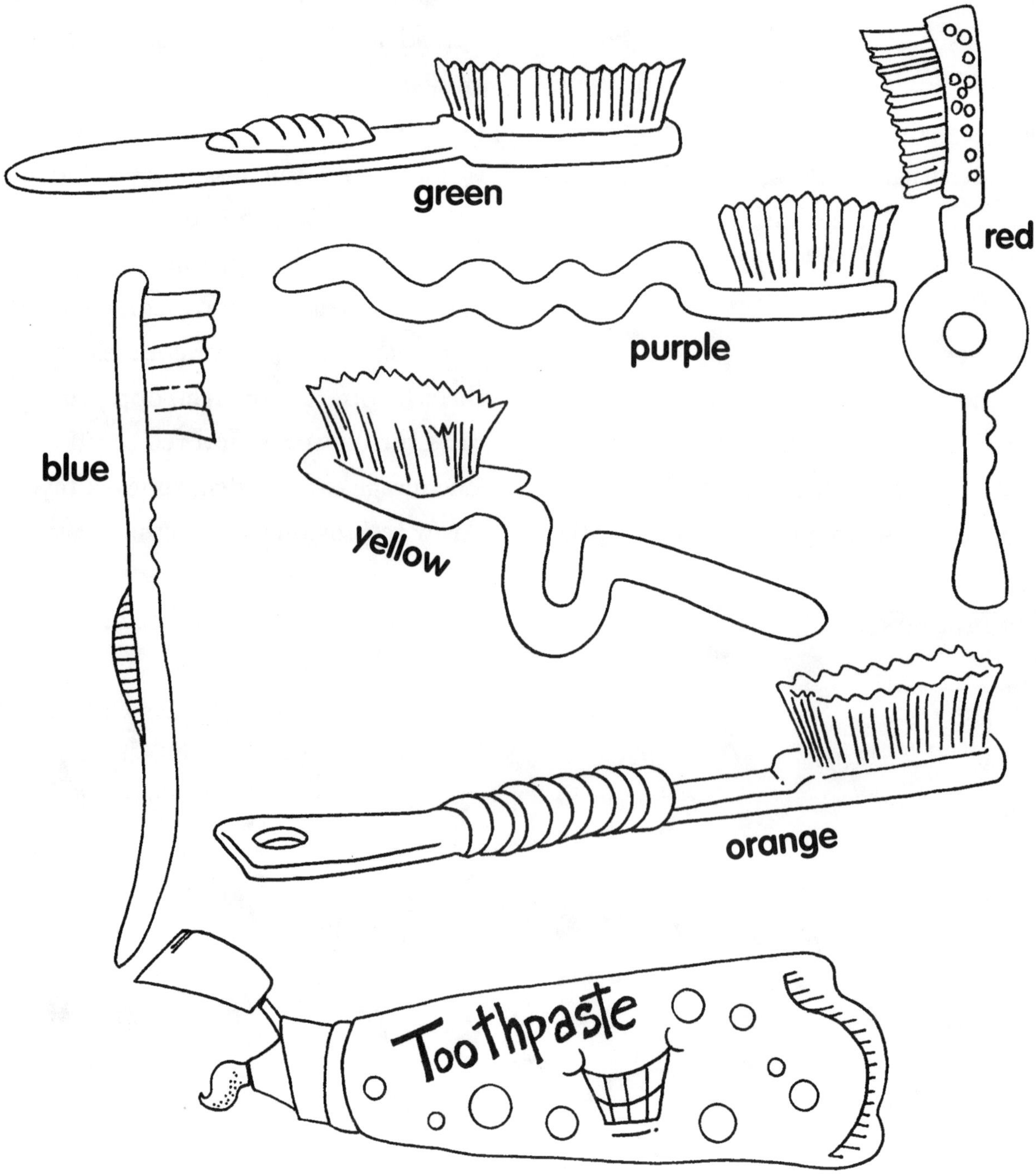

green

red

purple

blue

yellow

orange

14

© McGraw-Hill Children's Publishing

LL80006 *Personal Hygiene*

Lesson 2

Caring for Your Teeth

Objective: Student will be able to hold toothbrush correctly.

Explanation: Students often do not know how to hold and manipulate a toothbrush in order to brush their teeth. During this activity, students will practice holding and manipulating toothbrushes correctly.

Materials Needed:

- Toothbrush and toothpaste for each student
- Plastic or wax teeth (can be purchased from a party supply store or perhaps a discount chain store)
- Set of false teeth or dentist's impression of someone's teeth (A dentist will often allow you to borrow one.)

Directions to Teacher:

1.) Discuss with the students the fact that we have to hold many items according to their purpose. Ask them for examples, such as a pencil, scissors, and a baseball.

2.) Show the students a toothbrush. Explain to them that the toothbrush has a very special job to do. Compare the toothbrush with a broom which sweeps dirt off the floor. Let the students know that unbrushed teeth get ugly and smelly and gunky just like a dirty floor and can start to hurt a lot. (Brushing removes trapped food and plaque—a film of bacteria, saliva, and food particles.) Explain the concept of bacteria as little tiny bugs and cavities as the holes they dig in the teeth to have a place to live.

3.) Demonstrate to the students how to hold a toothbrush. Have each one practice this as you observe and offer assistance.

4.) Using plastic teeth or the teeth from the dentist, demonstrate how to use the toothbrush to brush teeth.

5.) Give each student plastic or wax teeth.

6.) Allow the students to practice the skill of applying toothpaste (see Lesson 1). Provide positive reinforcement when they accomplish this goal.

7.) Encourage the students to practice brushing the plastic/wax teeth.

8.) As the students brush the teeth, have them sing the following song (use the tune of "Row, Row, Row Your Boat"): "Brush, brush, brush your teeth. Brush your teeth each day. I know how to hold my brush to clean the dirt away." Encourage the students to synchronize their strokes with the beat of the song.

Caring for Your Teeth–Lesson 2

Salute Your Tooth

Circle the pictures which show the correct way to hold a toothbrush. Color the pictures.

Lesson 3

Caring for Your Teeth

Objective: Student will be able to brush his/her teeth according to dentists' therapeutic standards.

Explanation: Students do not usually know the proper method for brushing their teeth to prevent dental decay. This lesson will teach them the method recommended by dentists and hopefully promote better dental health.

Materials Needed:
- Toothbrush and toothpaste for each student
- False teeth or dental models
- Plastic or wax teeth
- Flash cards (see pages 18–23)
- A broom

Advance Preparation:
Photocopy and glue the flash cards onto poster board. Color them as desired.

Directions to Teacher:

1.) Use the broom to demonstrate that you cannot brush the floor free of dirt without holding the broom the correct way. Be as silly as possible to demonstrate the point.

2.) Discuss with the students how this is also true when brushing teeth. Remind them that they need to use toothbrushes in special ways to clean their teeth and remove the plaque/bacteria (little bugs) from their teeth.

3.) Show the flash cards while explaining the procedure for cleaning the teeth. Rephrase the accompanying instructions in language your students will understand. (Example: 45-degree angle could be said to be almost, but not quite all the way, sideways.)

4.) Demonstrate the correct way to clean teeth by brushing the teeth on the dental model with a dry toothbrush as you discuss the information on the flash cards.

5.) Encourage the students to practice the same brushing methods on the plastic or wax teeth.

6.) When appropriate, have the students practice on their own teeth without toothpaste. If necessary, use the flash cards and demonstrate the correct method for students who still need assistance. After cleaning their teeth, also have the students brush their tongues to remove bacteria and food particles.

7.) Allow the students to brush their teeth with toothpaste. As rewards, you may give the wax or plastic teeth to the students who brush their teeth correctly.

17

© McGraw-Hill Children's Publishing   LL80006 *Personal Hygiene*

Caring for Your Teeth

Lesson 3–Flash Card 1

Hold the tips of the bristles along the gumline at a 45–degree angle. Be sure the bristles touch both the tooth surface and the gumline.

© McGraw-Hill Children's Publishing

LL80006 *Personal Hygiene*

Caring for Your Teeth

Lesson 3–Flash Card 2

Move the brush in a back and forth rolling motion. Gently brush the outer tooth surfaces of the upper and lower jaw.

Caring for Your Teeth

Lesson 3–Flash Card 3

Hold the bristles at a 45–degree angle along the gumline. Gently brush the inner tooth surfaces using the same motion.

Caring for Your Teeth

Lesson 3–Flash Card 4

Tilt the brush against the inside surfaces of the front teeth. Use up and down motions to clean the teeth.

Caring for Your Teeth

Lesson 3–Flash Card 5

Brush the biting surface of all teeth.
Use a gentle back and forth motion.

Caring for Your Teeth

Lesson 3–Flash Card 6

Brush your tongue from back to front to remove bacteria. This will freshen your breath.

Name _____

Caring for Your Teeth–Lesson 3–Activity

Brushing in Line

Think about the steps for cleaning your teeth. Paste the pictures in the correct order below.

1	2
3	4
5	6

24

© McGraw-Hill Children's Publishing

LL80006 *Personal Hygiene*

Caring for Your Teeth

Lesson 3–Activity

Pictures for Brushing in Line

Cut out the pictures and paste them in the correct order on page 24.

Lesson 4

Caring for Your Teeth

Objective: Student will be able to floss his/her teeth correctly.

Explanation: Good dental hygiene requires the ability to floss teeth. Many students will not even know about the need to floss, much less how to proceed correctly. This lesson will familiarize them with the concept of flossing and teach them the proper steps.

Materials Needed:
- Several rolls of dental floss in different flavors and colors
- Flash cards (see pages 27–30)
- Small folded piece of paper
- A toothbrush
- Large mirror

Advance Preparation:
Photocopy and glue the flash cards onto poster board. Color them as desired.

Directions to Teacher:

1.) Give each student a piece of plain dental floss about 18 inches (46 cm) in length. Do not let the students see the dental floss container or let them know the lesson topic.

2.) Ask each student to think of one or more uses for this string. Give positive reinforcement for good ideas.

3.) After the students have shared their ideas, explain that this string has a very special purpose. Have one student hold a small piece of folded or rolled-up paper very tightly between the palms of his/her hands which are pressed against each other. Let another student try to use a toothbrush to get the paper out without hurting the first student, bending fingers back, brushing too hard, etc. Then use the piece of dental floss and slide it between the student's hands to bring out the piece of paper. (*Hint:* Practice this with a friend first to determine the right size of paper needed to demonstrate this technique successfully.)

4.) Explain that food sometimes becomes lodged between our teeth and the bacteria (little bugs) live on it and use the energy to make holes in our teeth which hurt. Explain that the dental floss can be used to remove the food that is caught between the teeth just like the paper which was held between the student's hands.

5.) Using the flash cards provided, explain how to use dental floss. Demonstrate with your hands as you explain the steps.

6.) Allow each student to practice each step as you explain it. Do not proceed to the next step until the students have practiced and thoroughly understand the step on which you are working.

7.) At step three, let each student practice between another student's hands or fingers several times before working on teeth. Caution them strongly to be gentle so as not to hurt the other person's hands.

8.) Before students use the floss on their own teeth, let them choose a color or flavor of floss that they like. Then, when the students have demonstrated flossing their teeth correctly, give a student a container of the kind of floss he/she likes as a reward.

© McGraw-Hill Children's Publishing   LL80006 *Personal Hygiene*

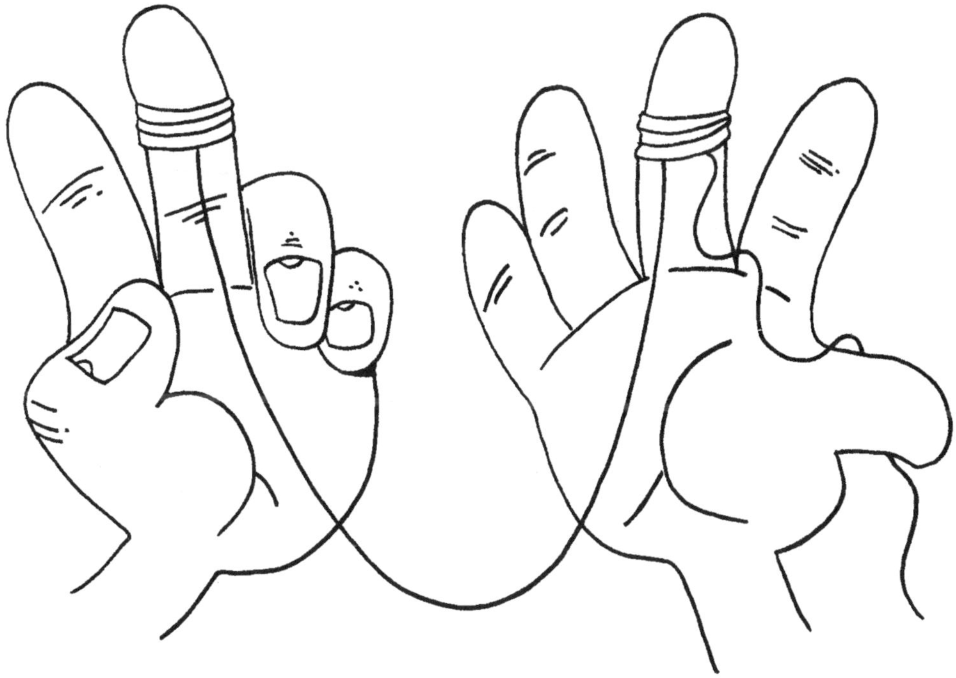

Caring for Your Teeth

Lesson 4–Flash Card 1

Break off about 18" (46 cm) of floss.
Wind most of it around the middle fingers of both hands.

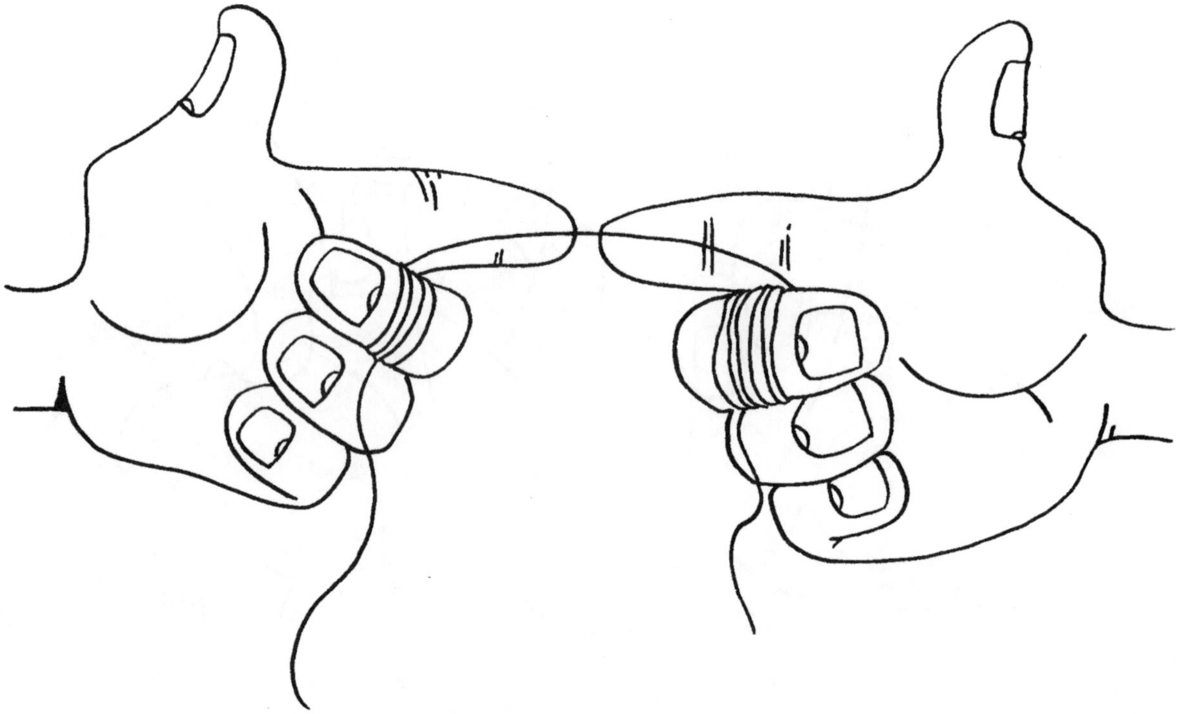

Caring for Your Teeth

Lesson 4–Flash Card 2

Use your index fingers to guide the floss between the teeth.

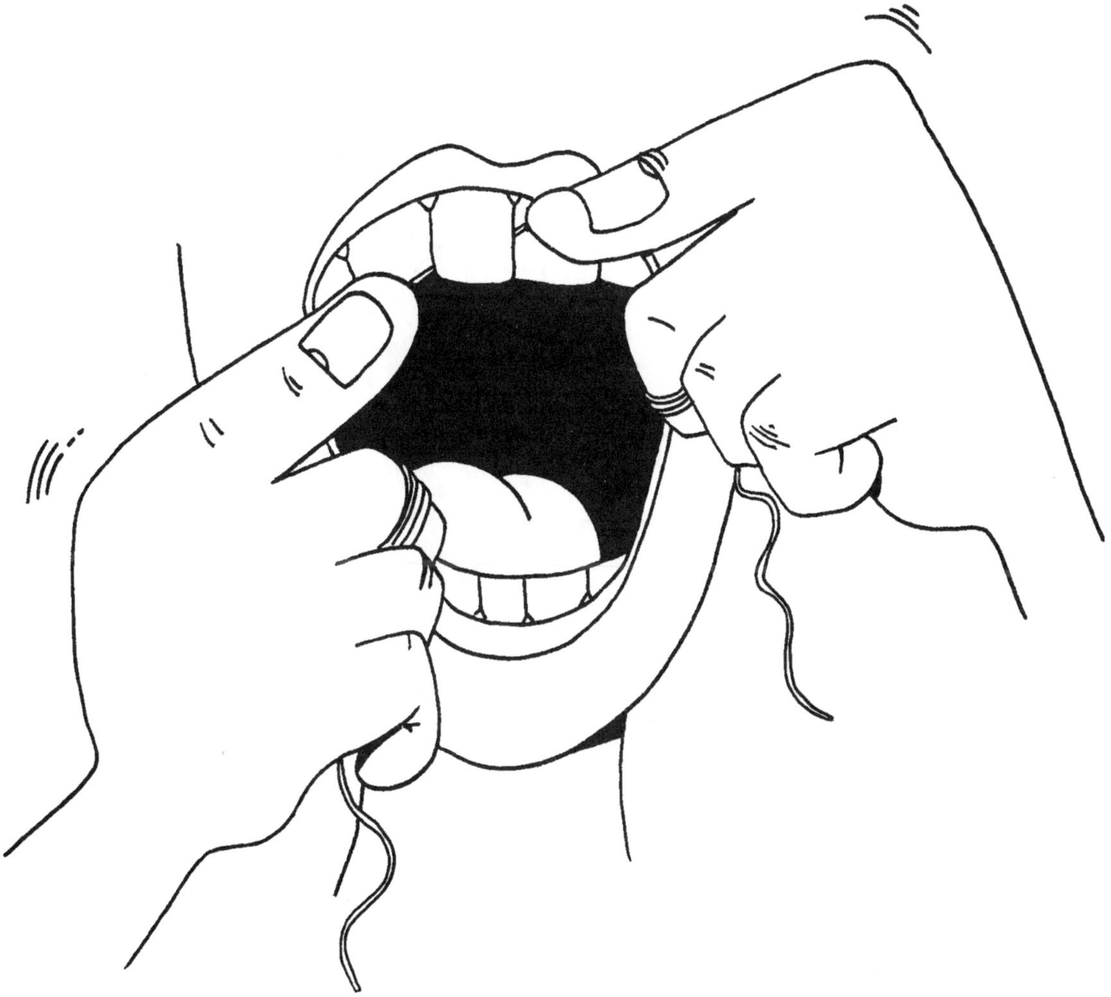

Caring for Your Teeth

Lesson 4—Flash Card 3

Slide the floss between the teeth using a gentle zig-zag motion. Hold the floss against the tooth to follow its shape.

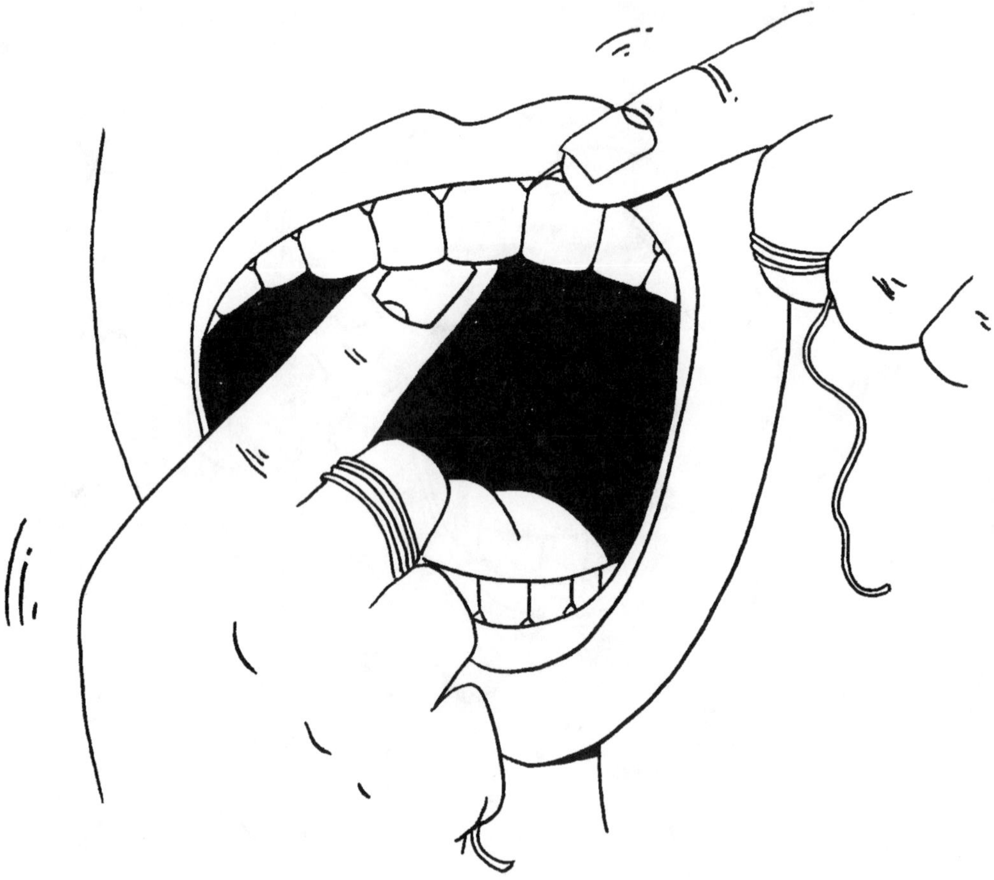

Caring for Your Teeth

Lesson 4–Flash Card 4

Move the floss up and down against the tooth surface and under the gumline. Floss each tooth with a clean part of the floss.

Name _____

Caring for Your Teeth–Lesson 4–Activity

Flossing the Right Way

Think about the steps for flossing your teeth.
Paste the pictures in the correct order.

1	2
3	4

© McGraw-Hill Children's Publishing — LL80006 *Personal Hygiene*

Caring for Your Teeth

Lesson 4–Activity

Pictures for Flossing the Right Way

Cut out the pictures below. Paste them in the correct order on page 31.

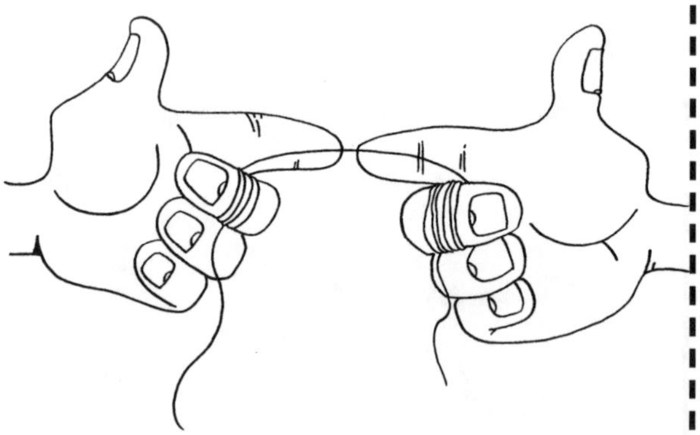

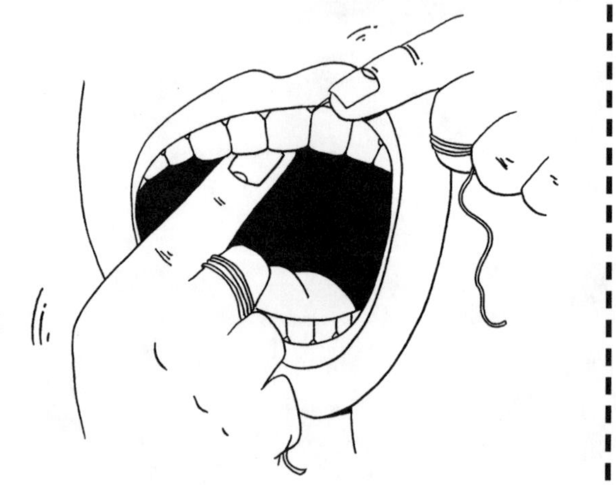

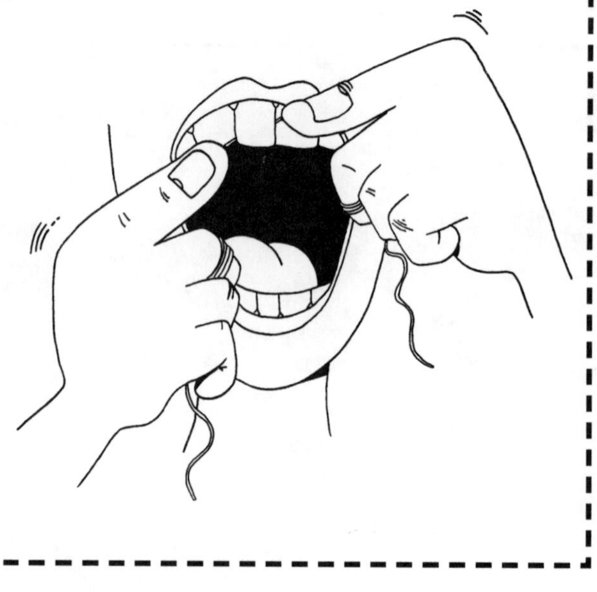

Lesson 1

Washing Your Hands

Objective: Student will be able to use the appropriate amount of soap to wash his/her hands correctly.

Explanation: Often, students use a great deal of soap or none at all. This activity will help them learn the importance of cleansing with soap and how much to use.

Materials Needed:
- A penny and paper towels
- Several small containers of different types of liquid hand soap
- A permanent fine-tipped marking pen
- Several bars of hand soap with various interesting fragrances and colors
- Access to a sink or several small pails of water

Directions to Teacher:

1.) Explain to the students the concept of germs as "tiny bugs" that live everywhere. Tell them that some of these little germs can make them very sick. Explain how the germs or teeny bugs can be on their hands and get into their mouths or noses or eyes and move on into their stomachs or up into their noses and then make them sick. Let them know that by washing their hands they can remove or kill these little bugs and will stay healthier.

2.) Tell the students that only a certain amount of soap is needed. Let them know that too much soap is very hard to rinse off and can make their hands dry or irritated or burn their eyes or nose if touched.

3.) First, show the students the bar of soap. Explain to the students that when they wash their hands with the soap they need to turn the bar of soap in their wet hands three times. Demonstrate this to them and let them practice with the dry soap. Have them count aloud individually and as a group "one, two, three," as they rotate the bar of soap in their hands.

4.) As the students complete this step correctly with the dry soap bar, encourage them to select a favorite bar of soap and practice the same step with water. Each student who does this correctly at least three times gets to keep his/her bar of soap.

5.) Now talk about how to use liquid soap. Draw a circle in the middle of each student's hand, using the penny as your pattern. Tell the students that they need to use that much liquid soap each time they wash their hands. Have the students practice putting that amount of liquid soap in their hands. (You may have to teach some students how to use the pump.) The students will need to wipe off the soap with paper towels after each try. When a student does this step correctly three times, she/he gets to choose a liquid soap and wash her/his hands with water. Save the liquid soap for the next activity.

© McGraw-Hill Children's Publishing   LL80006 *Personal Hygiene*

Name _____

Washing Your Hands–Lesson 1

Soapy Fun

Draw a line from the bar soap to the picture showing the correct number of times to turn the soap in your hands.

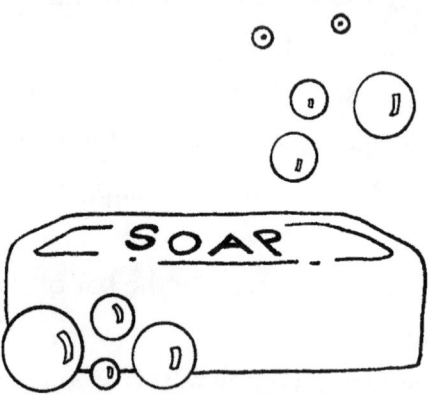

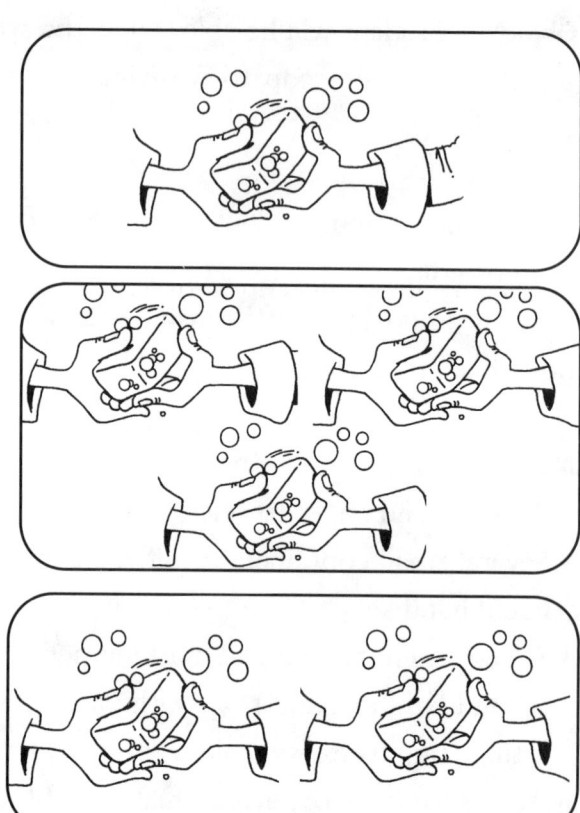

Draw a line from the liquid soap to the picture showing the correct amount to use.

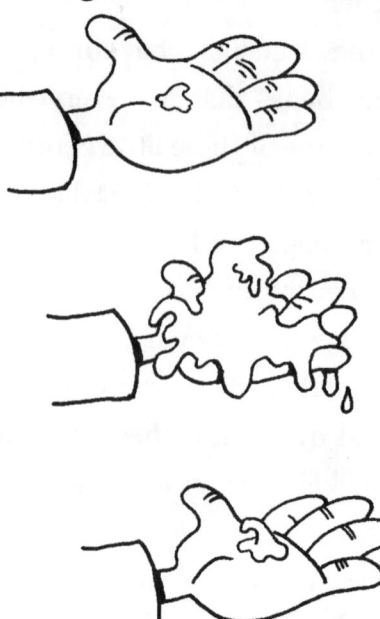

Lesson 2

Washing Your Hands

Objective: Student will be able to wash his/her hands correctly.

Explanation: Students often simply hold their hands under running water, if they attempt to wash them at all. This activity will help the students learn the correct technique to clean their hands thoroughly.

Materials Needed:
- Liquid soap from first activity
- Flash cards (see pages 36–41)
- Access to a sink or several pails of water

Advance Preparation:
Photocopy and glue the flash cards to poster board. Color them as desired.

Directions to Teacher:

1.) Remind the students about the need to cleanse their hands to remove the germs or little bugs that live on their skin.

2.) Using the provided flash cards, discuss with the students the steps for washing hands. It may be necessary to demonstrate by washing your own hands. (Use liquid soap for this activity, but remind the students about how they should use bar soap.)

3.) Have each student individually practice the activity as you observe and help as needed.

4.) Be sure to emphasize the need to rinse their hands thoroughly.

5.) As the students wash their hands, encourage them to sing the following song (use the tune of "Row, Row, Row Your Boat"): "Wash, wash, wash our hands; wash our hands always. Washing gets our hands so clean by washing germs away."

6.) Provide the first student to do this correctly an opportunity to select a bottle of liquid soap to keep. The second student who demonstrates this skill correctly may choose from the remaining bottles, and so on.

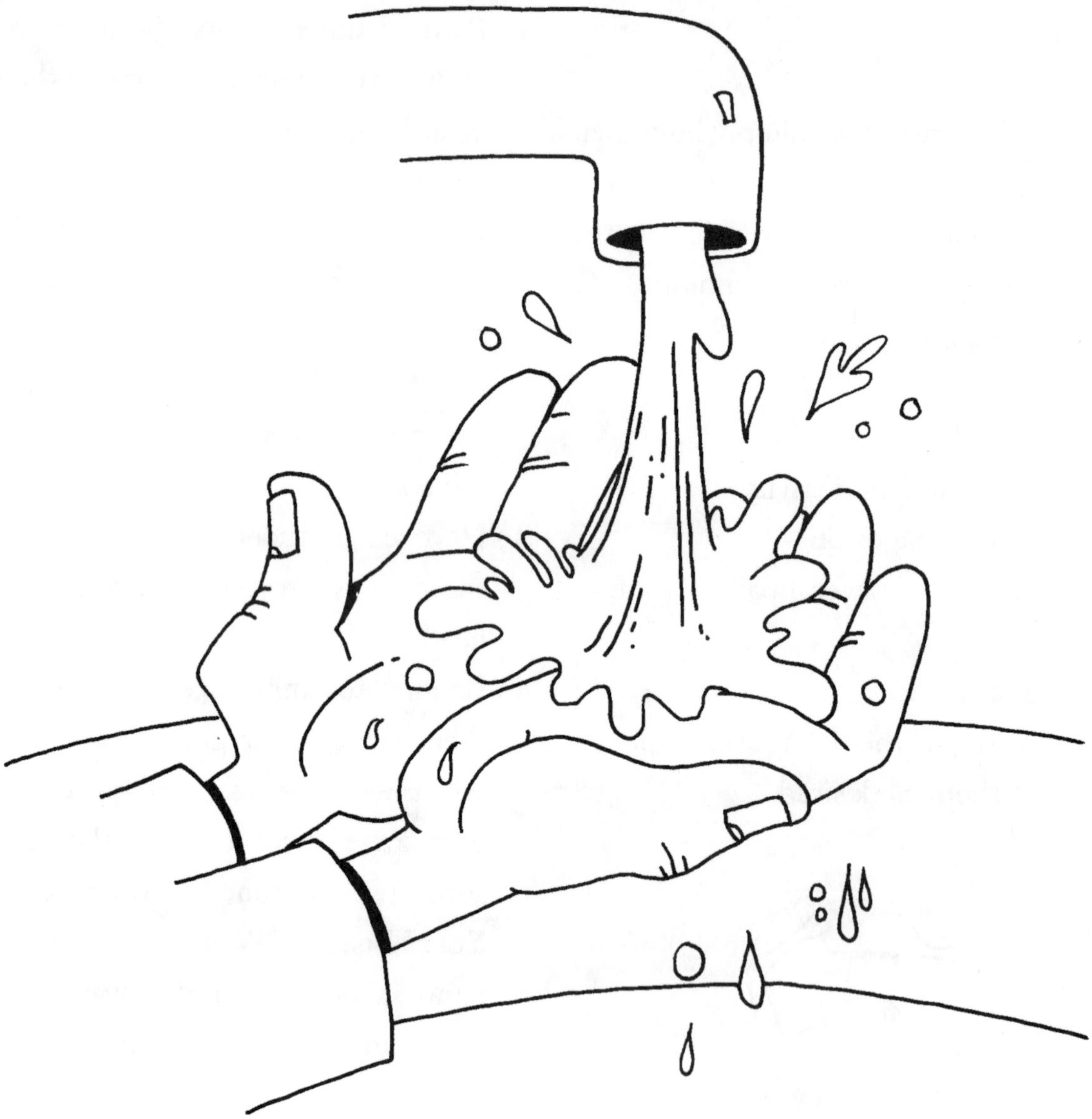

Washing Hands

Lesson 2—Flash Card 1

Wet your hands.

Washing Your Hands

Lesson 2–Flash Card 2

Put soap on your hands.

Washing Your Hands

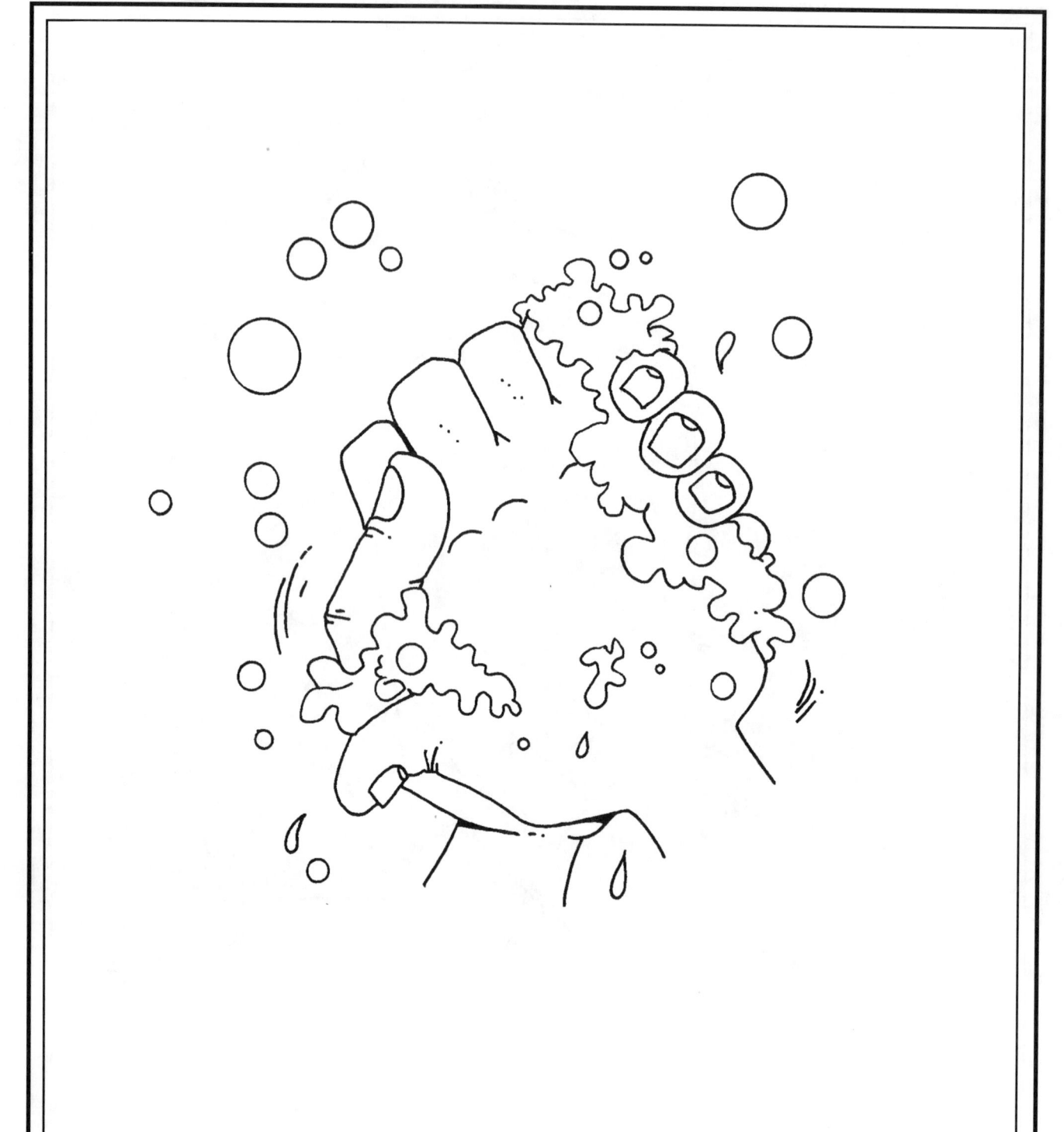

Lesson 2—Flash Card 3

Rub hands together, rubbing front and back two or three times to make a soapy lather.

© McGraw-Hill Children's Publishing

LL80006 *Personal Hygiene*

Washing Your Hands

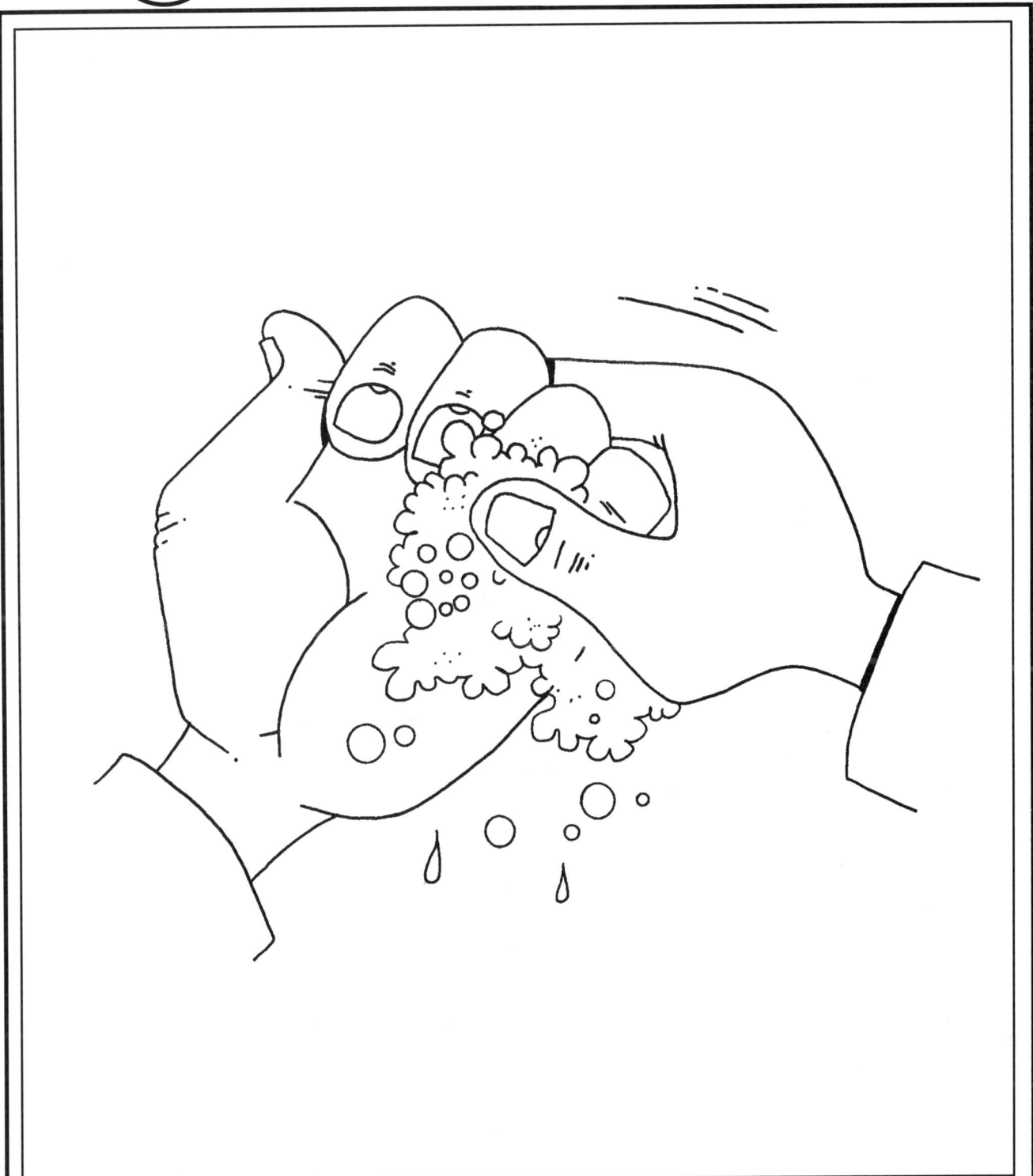

Lesson 2–Flash Card 4

Use the thumb of each hand to clean the fingernails and under the nails of the other hand.

Washing Your Hands

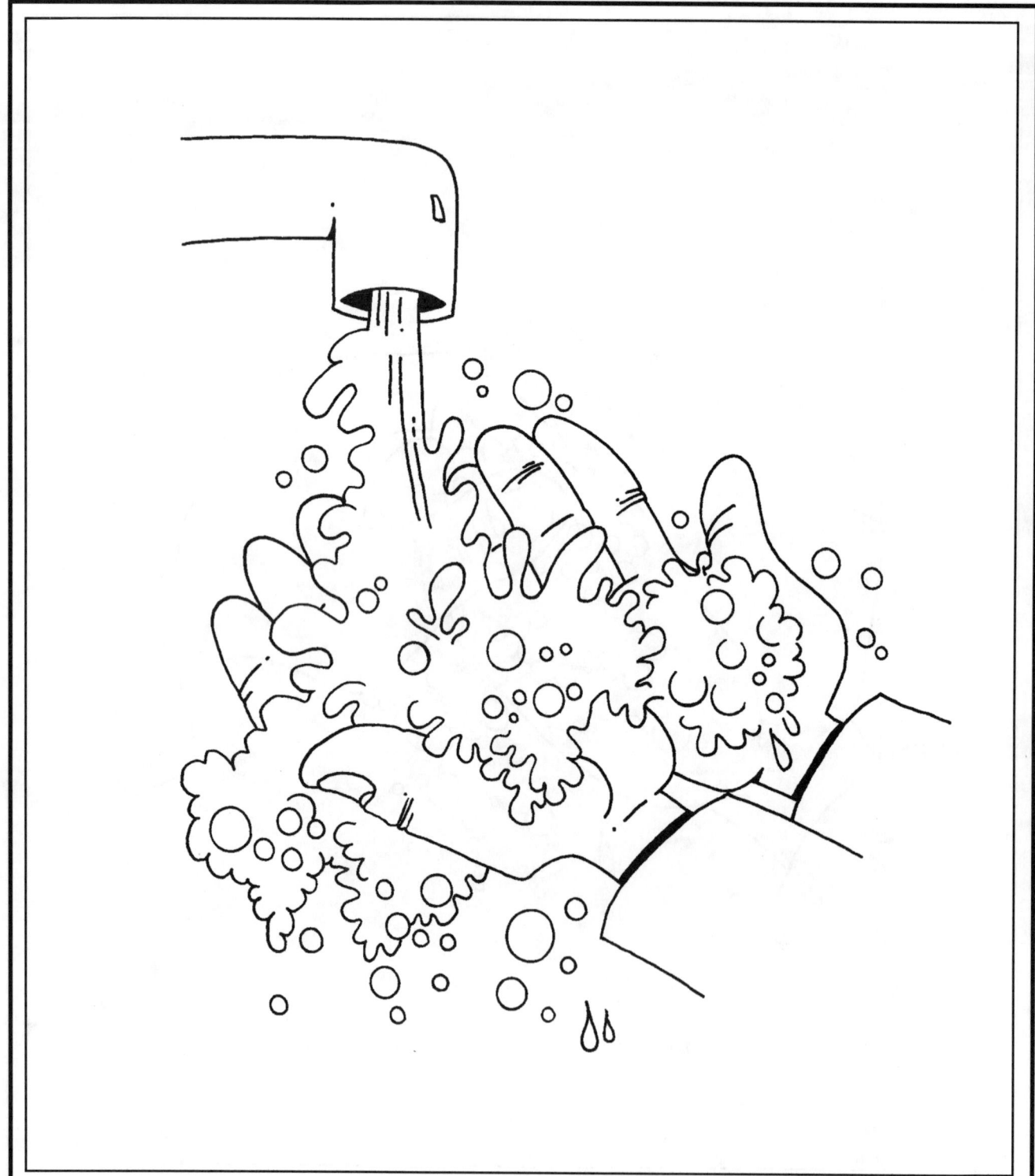

Lesson 2–Flash Card 5

Rinse your hands well under running water.

© McGraw-Hill Children's Publishing

LL80006 *Personal Hygiene*

Washing Your Hands

Lesson 2–Flash Card 6

Dry your hands well with a clean towel.

Name _____

Washing Your Hands—Lesson 2—Activity

Wash Away

Think about the steps to wash your hands properly. Paste the pictures in the correct order.

1	2
3	4
5	6

© McGraw-Hill Children's Publishing LL80006 *Personal Hygiene*

Washing Your Hands

Lesson 2–Activity

Pictures for Wash Away

Cut out the pictures. Paste them in the correct order on page 42.

Lesson 3

Washing Your Hands

Objective: Student will be able to determine when he/she needs to wash his/her hands.

Explanation: Students often do not know when and why to wash their hands and will not wash their hands at appropriate times (examples include: before eating and flossing or brushing teeth, or after using the restroom, petting the family pet, and blowing the nose). This activity will help students to identify specific situations when they need to wash their hands.

Materials Needed:
- Large sheet of chart paper
- Watercolor marker
- Magazines
- Scissors
- Glue or paste

Directions to Teacher:

1.) Lead the student in a discussion of why they wash their hands, reviewing the information shared during previous lessons about germs.

2.) Have the students identify situations when they think they should wash their hands. Record their ideas on the large sheet of chart paper. Give the students a great deal of positive reinforcement for their ideas. Let everyone decide as a group if each idea is appropriate and explain why or why not. Be careful to name at least a few times when they do not need to wash their hands so that obsessive hand washing is not encouraged. Examples include: when the students are going outside to play, when they are about to go to the store, or when they are going to clean up their rooms. You may consider making two lists if you do not think the lists will confuse your students.

3.) After completing the discussion, allow the students to finish the first activity sheet and then share their results with the group. If interested, display the papers on a large group bulletin board or as a collage.

Washing Your Hands–Lesson 3–Activity Sheet 1

Sticky Situations

Cut pictures out of magazines showing when you need to wash your hands. Glue them to this page. Share the sheet with your class.

Name _____

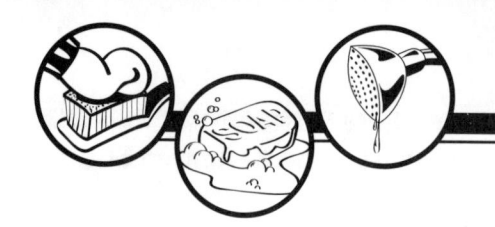

Washing Your Hands–Lesson 3–Activity Sheet 2

Wash Up

Draw a circle around each picture showing when you need to wash your hands.
Make a red X on each picture showing when you do not need to wash your hands.

Lesson 1

Washing Your Face

Objective: Student will understand the importance of using a washcloth.

Explanation: Students often cannot wash correctly because they do not understand the importance of using washcloths. This activity will teach them why a washcloth is important to use.

Materials Needed:

- Washcloth for each student (Try to have various colors and patterns.)
- Chalk or powder blush
- Light-colored lipstick
- Facial bar soap
- Access to a sink or several pails of water
- Magic marker
- Large sheet of chart paper
- Magazines
- Scissors
- Glue or paste

Directions to Teacher:

1.) Remind the students about the germs or little bugs that you discussed earlier. Explain to them that those little bugs also get on their faces along with dirt.

2.) Explain to the students that when we wash our faces we need to use our washcloths in order to clean the little bugs off really well. Let them know that the cloth is a little rough which cleans the skin better than by using only your hands.

3.) Let the students each choose a washcloth and then gently rub their faces with the dry cloths to feel the texture.

4.) Make a light chalk mark or brush some blush on their arms. Have the students try to remove the marks with their fingers using one quick rub. Then have them use the dry cloth to wipe the marks off and see how much better the cloth works. (You may need to experiment with the chalk or blush to find out how much should be applied to make your point. *Note:* Blush actually works better than chalk, if you have some.)

5.) Next apply a small amount of light-colored lipstick on their arms. Encourage the students to wipe off the lipstick with the dry cloths. Then, wet the washcloths and put some soap on them. Now have the students wash the lipstick off their arms. (Beforehand, experiment with how dark a mark of lipstick is needed.)

6.) Discuss how much better the wet, soapy cloth worked.

7.) Move from this demonstration into a discussion about when it is appropriate to use a washcloth. (Some examples are when your face is very greasy and when you are very dirty all over.) Give positive reinforcement for good answers.

© McGraw-Hill Children's Publishing LL80006 *Personal Hygiene*

Name _____

Washing Your Face–Lesson 1–Activity

Using a Washcloth

Cut pictures from magazines that show when you need to use a washcloth. Glue them on this page. If interested, show your page to a friend.

Name _____

Washing Your Face–Lesson 1–Activity

Wishy-Washy

Draw lines to match the hands with the pictures showing when to wash your hands.
Then draw lines to match the washcloth with the pictures showing when to use a washcloth.

Lesson 2

Washing Your Face

Objective: Student will be able to use the correct amount of soap on a washcloth.

Explanation: Students often use too much or not enough soap to cleanse themselves adequately. This activity will help them learn how much soap is needed on the washcloth.

Materials Needed:
- Washcloths from Lesson 1
- Liquid soap and bar soap
- Access to sink or several pails of water
- Permanent fine-tipped marker
- A penny and paper towels

Directions to Teacher:

1.) Remind the students of the activity in which they learned the correct amount of soap to use to wash their hands. Let them tell you what they learned and give positive reinforcement to the students who remember.

2.) Explain to the students that the same concept applies when using a washcloth. Let them know why too much soap is harmful (the soap cannot be rinsed out of the cloth well enough to rinse the body clean and soap residue can cause itching) and why too little soap is not helpful (will not clean the skin adequately).

3.) Tell the students that they can use the same amount of soap on their washcloths that they use on their hands.

4.) Allow each student to choose a washcloth. Use the penny and marker to draw a circle in the middle of the cloth. Let students practice applying the correct amount of liquid soap on their dry cloths. Use the paper towels to wipe the liquid soap off until they have done it correctly three times.

5.) After each student uses the correct amount of liquid soap on a dry cloth three times, allow him/her to practice with a wet cloth.

6.) When the students understand how to use a wet cloth, demonstrate how to rub the soap into the cloth. Then encourage the student to repeat this step as you observe. Give positive reinforcement when a student is successful.

7.) Demonstrate how to rinse the cloth well. Show the students how the cloth will not be stiff or have soap bubbles on it when it is rinsed thoroughly. Encourage the students to practice rinsing their cloths and squeezing out excess water after rinsing.

8.) Repeat the above steps by practicing with bars of soap. Have the students turn the bars of soap on their wet cloths three times, just as they did when washing their hands. Count aloud as a group—"one, two, three"—with each turn of the soap.

9.) Again, practice rinsing the cloths and their bodies well. Allow the students who have mastered this skill to keep their washcloths.

Name _____

Washing Your Face–Lesson 2

Wash Me!

Draw a circle around the washcloth holding the correct amount of liquid soap. Color and decorate the washcloth.

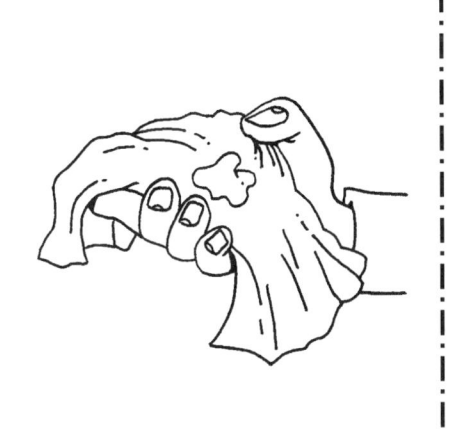

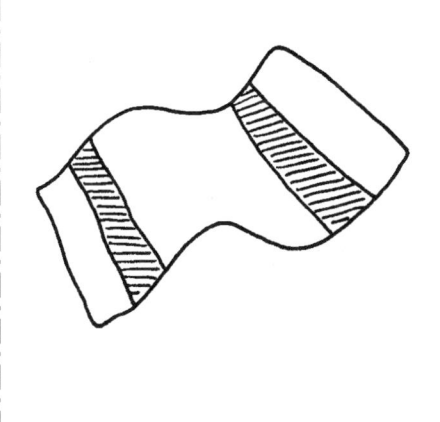

Draw a circle around the group of washcloths showing the hands turning the soap the correct number of times.

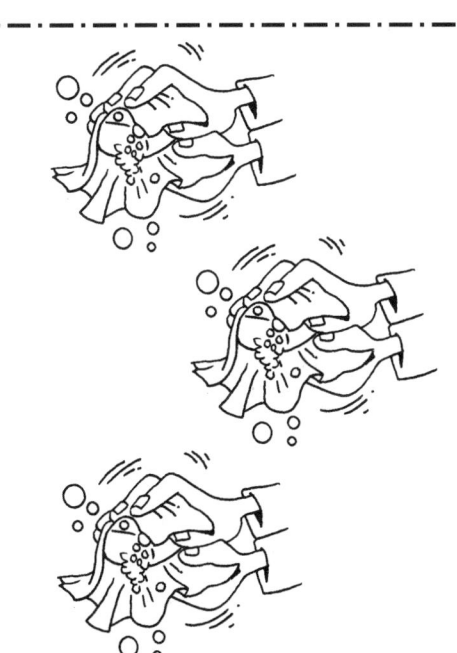

51

© McGraw-Hill Children's Publishing

LL80006 *Personal Hygiene*

Lesson 3

Washing Your Face

Objective: Student will wash face correctly.

Explanation: Students often only wash part of their faces if they wash them at all. They may also get soap in their eyes and ears. This activity will teach them how to wash their faces properly.

Materials Needed:
- Flash cards (see pages 53–60)
- Washcloths
- Soap
- Plastic dolls (one for each student)
- Access to sink or several pails of water
- Mirrors (one for each group of two or three students)

Advance Preparation:
Photocopy and glue the flash cards to poster board. Color them as desired.

Directions to Teacher:

1.) Remind the students about the lessons on soaping washcloths and removing the dirt, grease, and germs or little bugs that are on their faces.

2.) Using the flash cards and one of the dolls, discuss and demonstrate the steps for washing the face.

3.) Alert the students about the need to be careful when applying soap around their eyes and in their ears.

4.) Let the students practice each step on the plastic dolls. Observe how they handle the procedure and offer positive reinforcement as they complete each step correctly. First practice as a group and then allow the students to practice the skill individually.

5.) After the students have practiced successfully on dolls, allow them to use the mirrors and practice on themselves.

6.) Have each student demonstrate in front of the other students how to wash his/her face.

7.) Encourage the students to sing the following song as they practice. (Use the melody of "Here We Go 'Round the Mulberry Bush.") "Watch us learn to wash our faces, wash our faces, wash our faces. Now we learn to wash our faces so we will look real 'PURTY'."

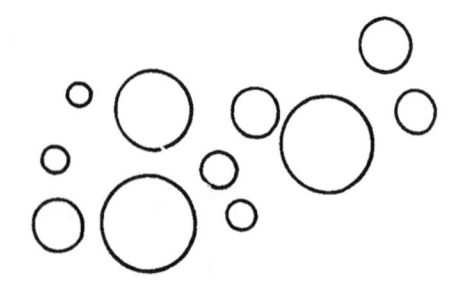

© McGraw-Hill Children's Publishing

LL80006 *Personal Hygiene*

Washing Your Face

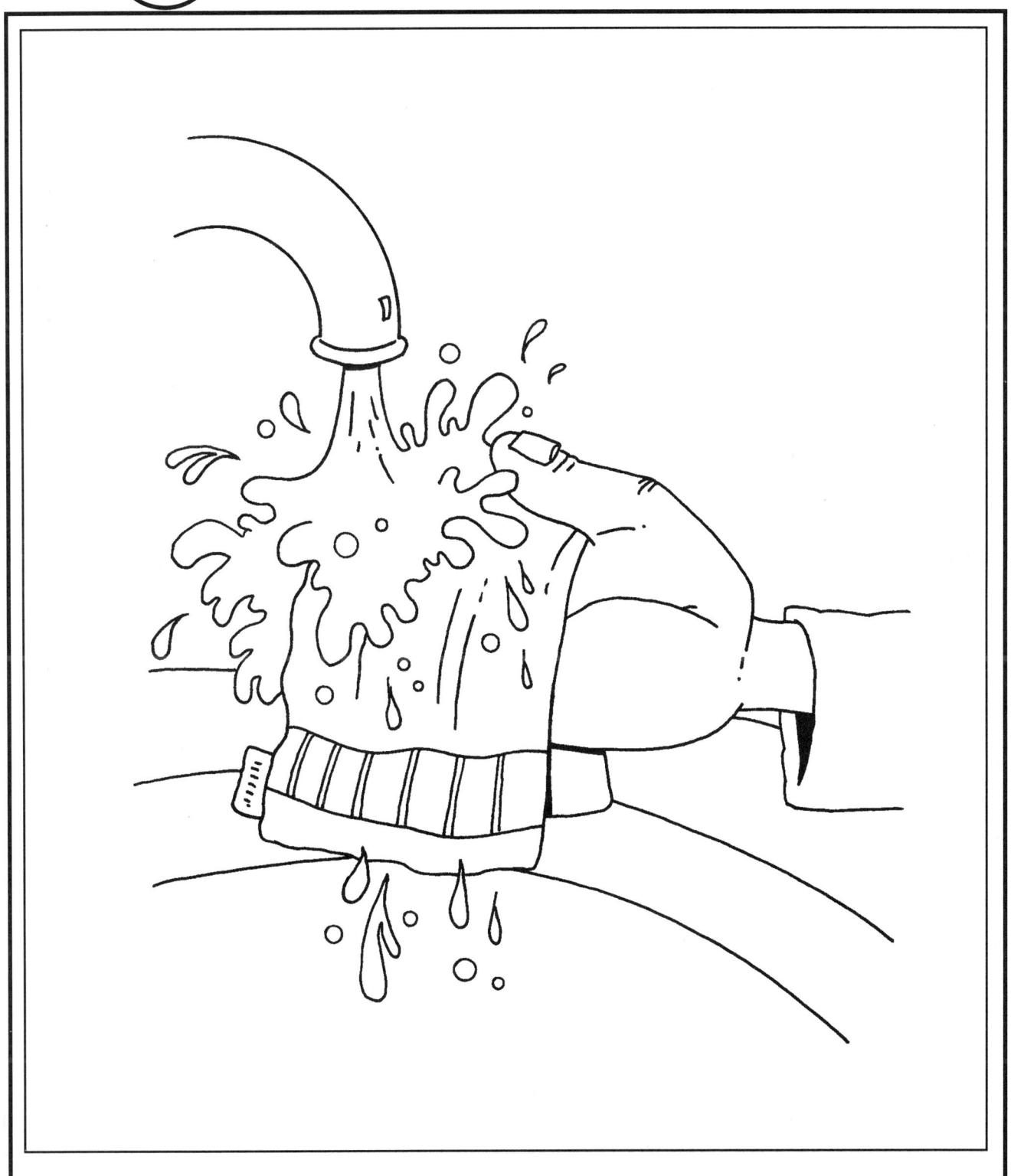

Lesson 3–Flash Card 1

Wet cloth and wipe face with it.

53

© McGraw-Hill Children's Publishing LL80006 *Personal Hygiene*

Washing Your Face

Lesson 3–Flash Card 2

Put soap on cloth.

© McGraw-Hill Children's Publishing

LL80006 *Personal Hygiene*

Washing Your Face

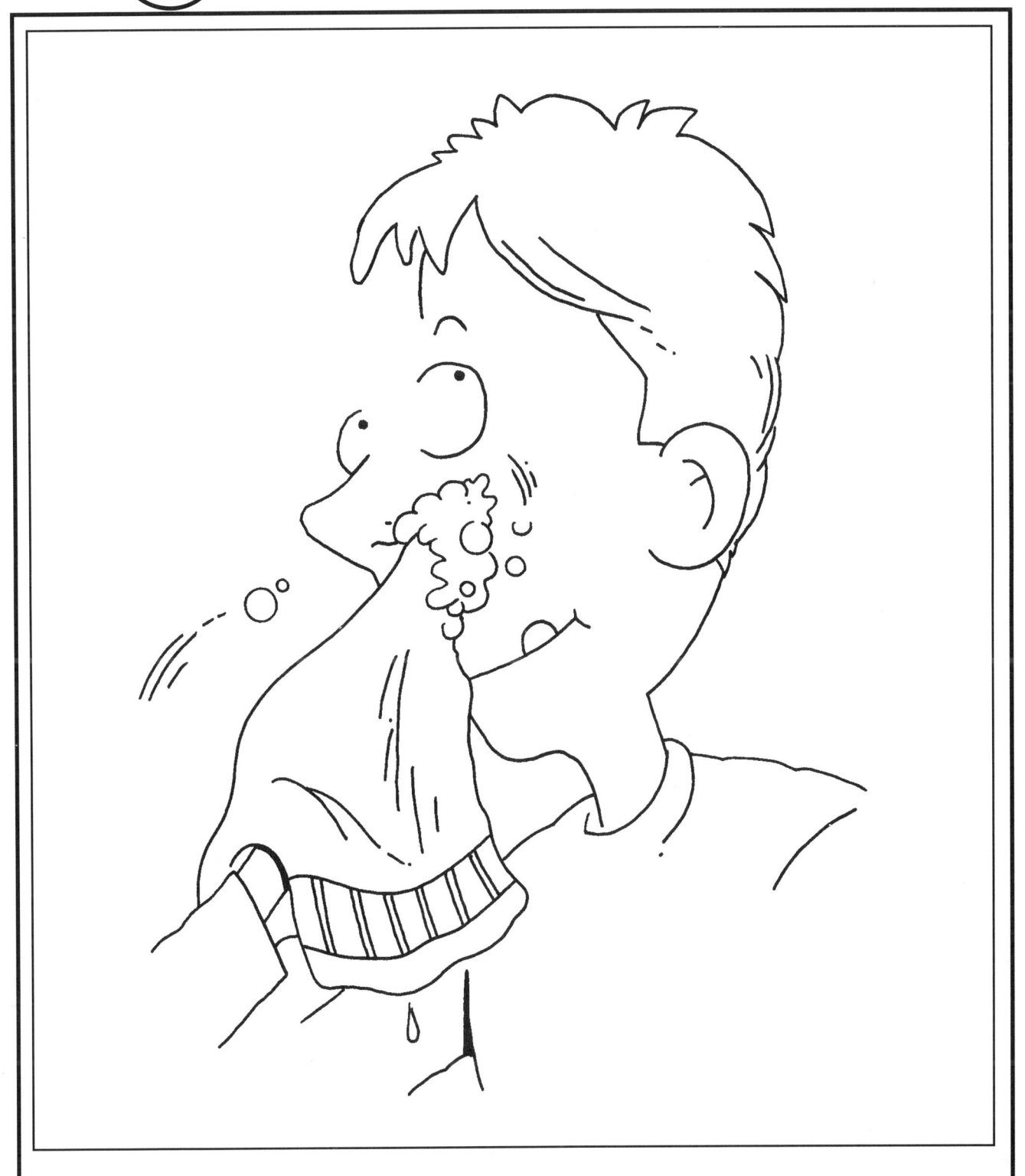

Lesson 3—Flash Card 3

Wash carefully around your eyes.

Washing Your Face

Lesson 3–Flash Card 4

Rinse cloth well and carefully wipe around eyes with rinsed cloth. Close eyes and work from edge of nose toward sides of face.

Washing Your Face

Lesson 3–Flash Card 5

Soap the cloth again.

Washing Your Face

Lesson 3—Flash Card 6

Wash the rest of your face and neck.

Washing Your Face

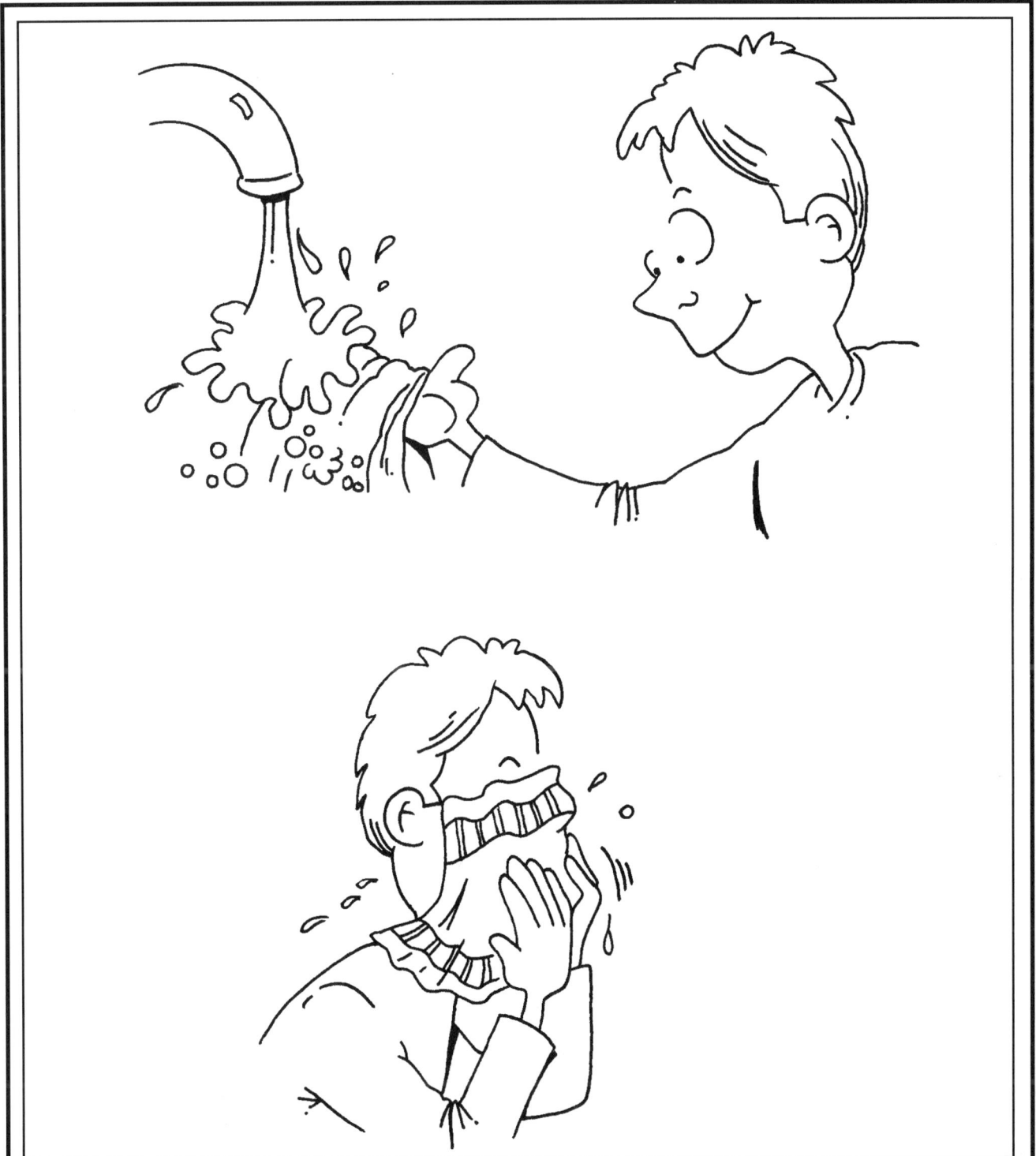

Lesson 3–Flash Card 7

Rinse the cloth well.
Wipe off face and neck with cloth two times.

Washing Your Face

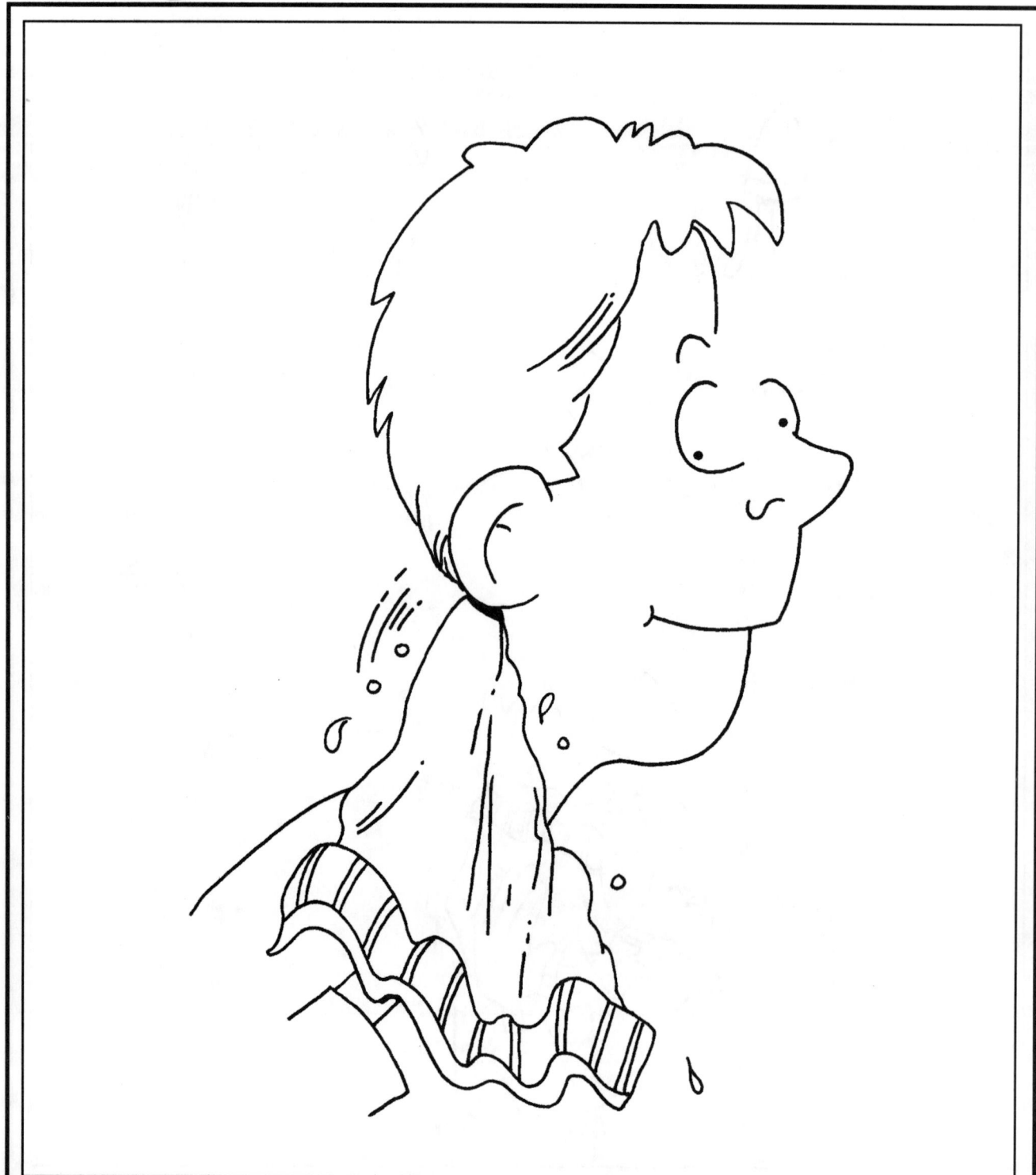

Lesson 3—Flash Card 8

Use wet, rinsed cloth to wipe around, behind, and inside earlobes.

Name _____

Washing Your Face–Lesson 3–Activity

A Clean Face

Think about the steps to wash your face properly. Paste the pictures in the correct order on this page.

1	2
3	4
5	6
7	8

© McGraw-Hill Children's Publishing

LL80006 *Personal Hygiene*

Washing Your Face

Lesson 3–Activity

Pictures for a Clean Face

Cut out the pictures below. Then paste them in the correct order on page 61.

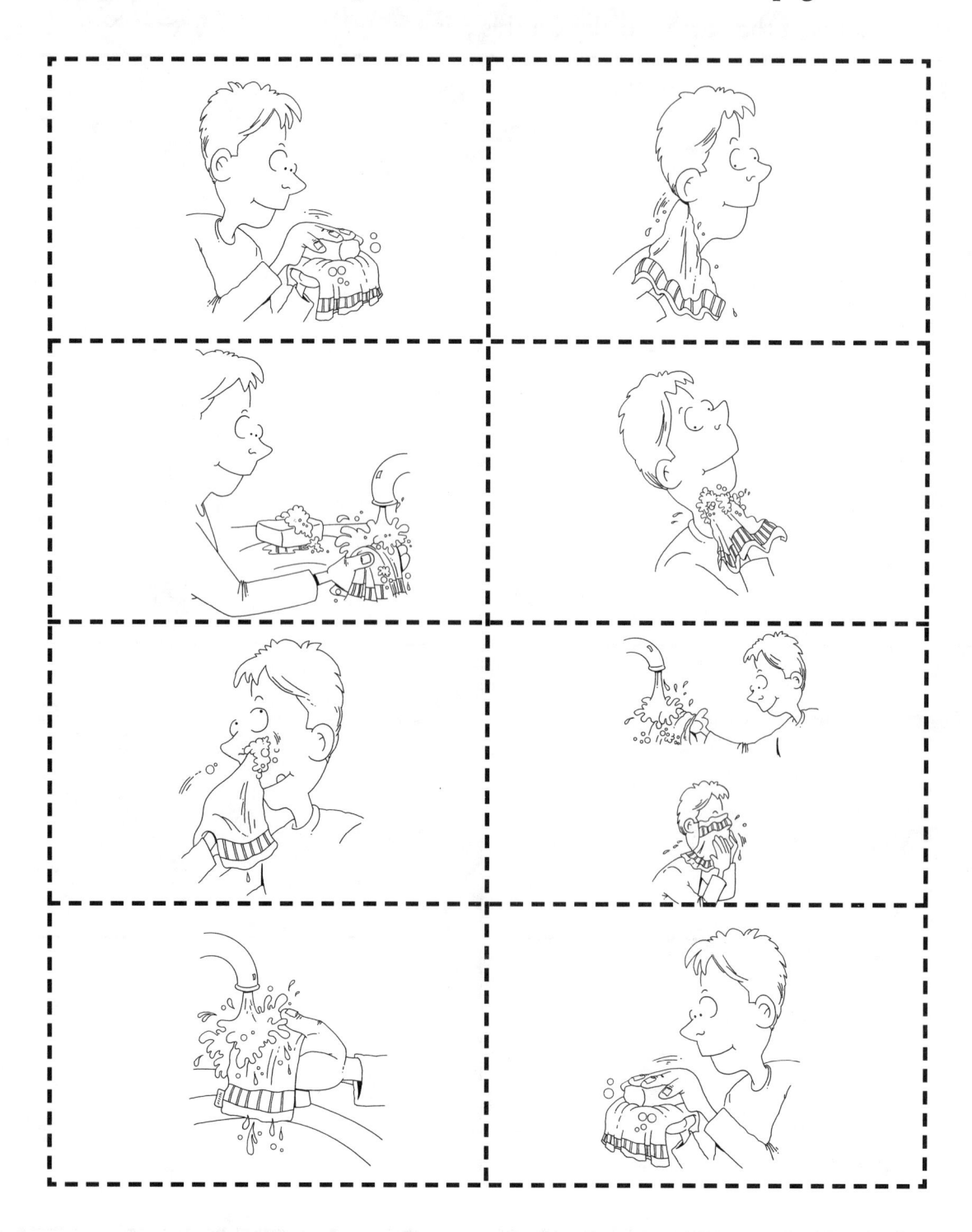

Lesson 1

Bathing Your Body

Objective: Student will be able to identify areas of his/her body that need extra bathing care.

Explanation: Students often do not understand that several areas of their body grow more bacteria, smell worse, and therefore need extra care. This activity will help them to realize that fact and identify which areas of the body need some extra hygienic care.

Materials Needed:
- Plastic dolls (one for each student)
- Paintbrush (one per student)
- Watercolor paints
- Large picture of cartoon character (see pages 64–65)

Advance Preparation:
Photocopy the cartoon character pattern pages. Tape the sections together at the character's waist. You may want to glue the picture onto heavier paper and color it.

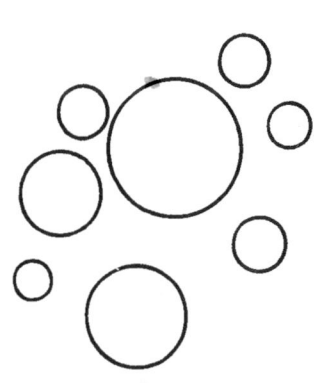

Directions to Teacher:

1.) Remind the students of your discussions about the germs or little bugs that live everywhere.

2.) Let them know that the little bugs love to grow in wet, dark places.

3.) Tell the students that the areas where little bugs grow a lot may become very smelly.

4.) Ask the students if they can guess where on the body the little bugs grow and make things very smelly. Use the large picture of the cartoon character's body and point to the areas that each student guesses. Mark the areas lightly with a pencil. Let the students vote on which areas they think bacteria grow the most. Lead them to eventually identify the underarms, the feet, and the private parts (front and back genital areas).

5.) Paint these areas on the large picture with a bright color of paint.

6.) Have the students paint on the plastic dolls where the smelly areas are. Offer much positive reinforcement for identifying the correct areas.

7.) Explain to the students that these areas need extra care when bathing.

© McGraw-Hill Children's Publishing

LL80006 *Personal Hygiene*

Bathing Your Body–Lesson 1–Figure

Bathing Beauty

Bathing Your Body–Lesson 1–Figure

Bathing Your Body–Lesson 1–Activity

Eew! Time for a Bath

Using a bright color crayon, color the smelly areas of the body.

Lesson 2

Bathing Your Body

Objective: Student will be able to understand and verbalize steps of applying soap to the washcloth, washing the body, and rinsing while bathing—both the cycle and the importance of each step.

Explanation: Often students do not realize the importance of using soap and/or the importance of rinsing well. They also do not grasp the bathing cycle of using soap, washing well, and rinsing thoroughly. This activity will help them to understand this process.

Materials Needed:
- Soap, wash, rinse chart on page 68
- Glass mirror
- Washcloth
- Bar soap
- Water in a pail
- Tempera paint and paintbrush

Directions to Teacher:

1.) In front of the students, paint a big stripe of brightly colored tempera paint on the mirror. Allow the paint to dry. Show the students that the mirror cannot be used with the paint on it.

2.) Try to wash the mirror with dry and damp cloths. Show the students how this procedure simply smears the paint; the mirror still cannot be used.

3.) Use soap to wash the paint off but do not rinse the mirror. Let it dry. Show the students the mirror which has a dry film on it. Talk about how the mirror is still useless.

4.) Rinse the mirror well. Let it dry. Show the students how the mirror is now usable. (You might have to experiment with how much paint and soap to use to make this demonstration effective.)

5.) Lead the students in a discussion about how our bodies are like the mirror and need to be soaped, washed, and rinsed to get really clean. Utilize the chart during this discussion to help the students understand this concept.

6.) Teach the students the following song to help them remember (use the tune of "Rawhide"): "Soap, wash, and rinse. Soap, wash, and rinse. Soap, wash, and rinse to get clean. That's what we have to do to clean our bodies well. We soap, wash, and rinse to get clean."

Bathing Your Body

Lesson 2–Chart

1, 2, 3, Clean As Can Be!

1

2

3

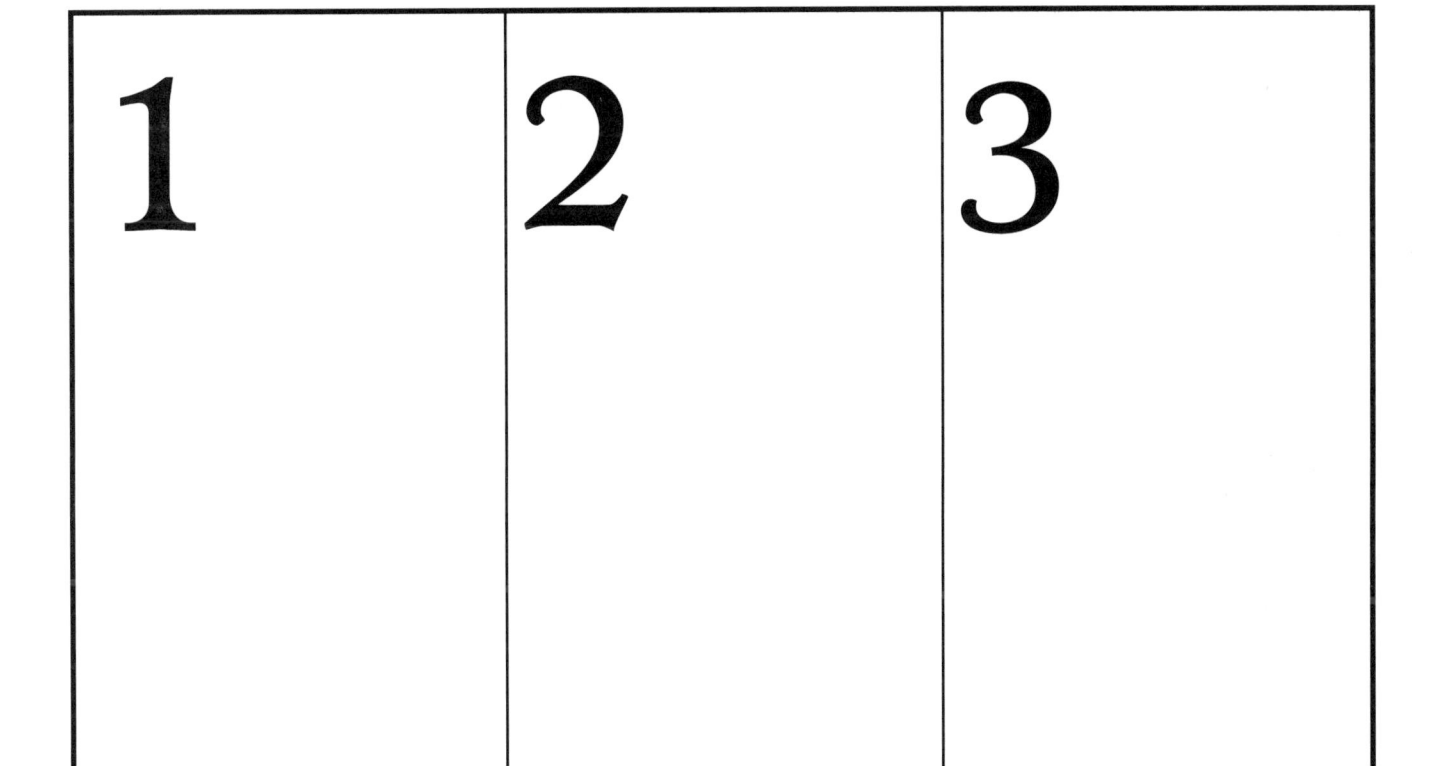

Bathing Your Body–Lesson 2–Activity

It's So Easy to Be Clean!

Color and cut out the pictures along the bottom of the page. Use glue or paste to put them in the correct order in the boxes.

1	2	3

Lesson 3

Bathing Your Body

Objective: Student will learn to wash each area of his/her body.

Explanation: Many students only spot wash their bodies, missing places or washing one area over and over again. This exercise will teach them to wash their entire bodies.

Materials Needed:
- Flash cards (see pages 71–76)
- Plastic doll and newspaper or vinyl tablecloth, for each student
- Soap, washcloth, and pan of water for each student

Advance Preparations:
Photocopy and glue the flash cards to poster board. Color them as desired.

Directions to Teacher:

1.) Cover each desk with vinyl tablecloth.
2.) Remind the students about the discussions you have had regarding germs and smelly body parts.
3.) Review the steps when cleaning the body: soap, wash, and rinse. (You may be interested in displaying the charts from the previous two activities as prompts during the discussions.)
4.) Discuss with the students the fact that to clean their bodies thoroughly—dirt and germ free—they have to soap, wash, and rinse every part of their body, especially the smelly parts.
5.) Utilizing the flash cards provided and demonstrating on a doll as you go, show the students the order to use to make sure every part of their bodies gets washed. Tell them that they will start at the top and move down, saving their private parts for last.
6.) Remind them that every part has to be soaped, washed, and rinsed to get it clean.
7.) After you have demonstrated what to do, have them each wash a doll. At first, do this step by step as a group. Then allow the students to practice individually, observing and offering help as needed.
8.) Finally, using the doll, have each student demonstrate to the group how to bathe properly.
9.) Sing the following song while they practice (use the tune of "Here We Go 'Round the Mulberry Bush"). First verse: "I take a bath every day, every day, every day. I take a bath every day to keep my body clean." Second verse: "First, I wash my face and neck, face and neck, face and neck. First, I wash my face and neck to get my body clean." Third verse: "Second, I wash my shoulders, arms, and hands, . . . etc." Fourth verse: "Third, I wash my underarms, . . . etc." Fifth verse: "Fourth, I wash my chest, stomach, and back, . . . etc. Sixth verse: "Fifth, I wash my legs and feet, . . . etc. Seventh verse: "Last, I wash my private parts, . . . etc.

© McGraw-Hill Children's Publishing

LL80006 *Personal Hygiene*

Bathing Your Body

Lesson 3–Flash Card 1

Wash face and neck like you learned before.
Be sure to close your eyes when needed.
Do not forget the back of your neck and behind your ears.

© McGraw-Hill Children's Publishing

LL80006 *Personal Hygiene*

Bathing Your Body

Lesson 3—Flash Card 2

Wash shoulders, arms, and hands.
Do not forget to wash between your fingers.

Bathing Your Body

Lesson 3–Flash Card 3

Wash underarms two times.
Make sure you get them good and clean.

© McGraw-Hill Children's Publishing

LL80006 *Personal Hygiene*

Bathing Your Body

Lesson 3—Flash Card 4

Wash chest, stomach, and back.
Make sure to wash your belly button.

Bathing Your Body

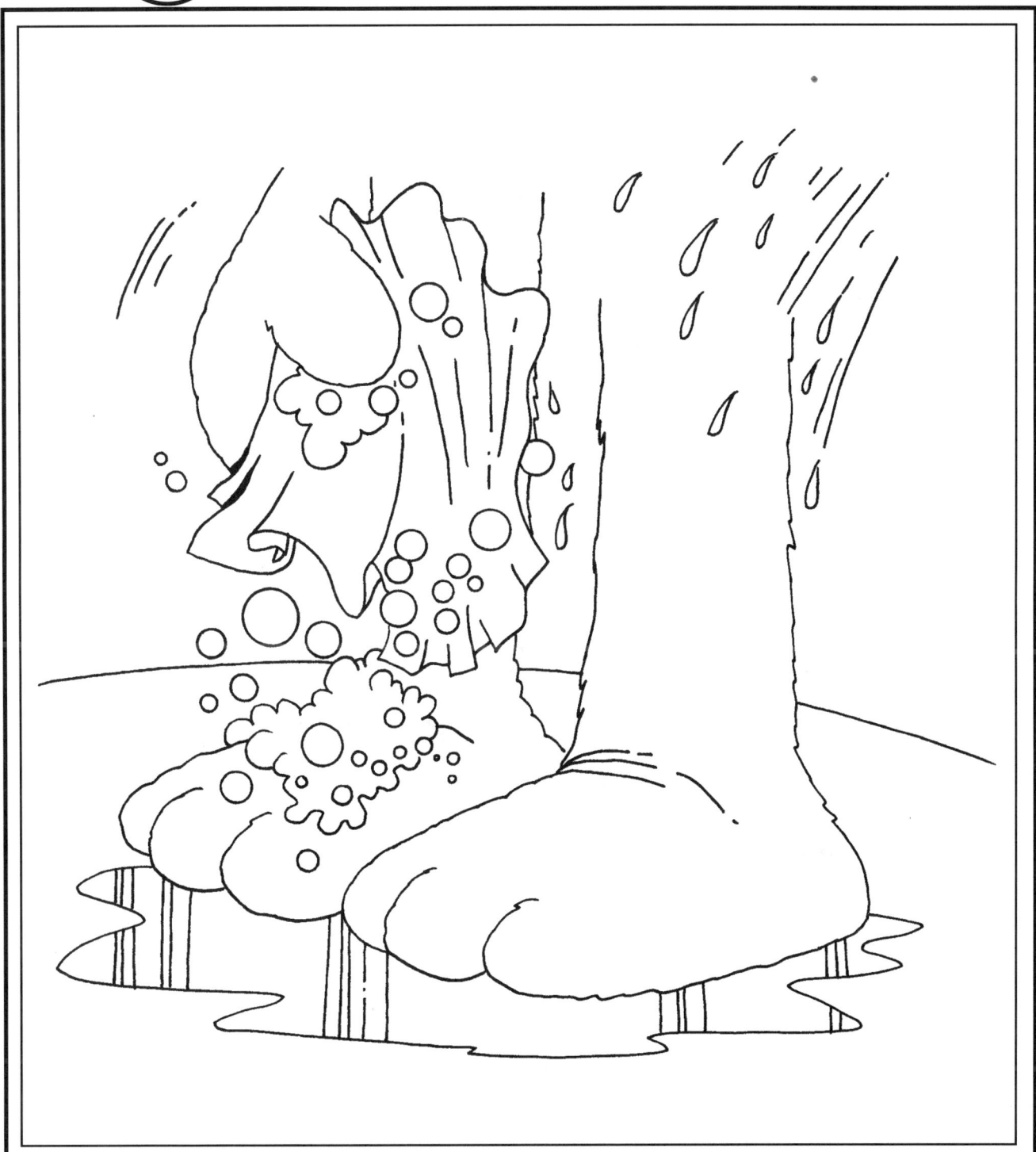

Lesson 3—Flash Card 5

Wash legs and feet. Wash feet twice and make sure to get between your toes.

Bathing Your Body

Lesson 3–Flash Card 6

Wash private parts. Make sure to get front and back. Be very gentle and be sure to rinse well.

Name _____

BATHING YOUR BODY–Lesson 3–Activity

Completely Clean!

Think about the steps to bathe your body properly.
Paste the pictures in the boxes in the correct order.

1	2
3	4
5	6

© McGraw-Hill Children's Publishing

LL80006 *Personal Hygiene*

Bathing Your Body

Lesson 3—Activity

Pictures for Completely Clean!

Cut out the pictures below. Paste them in the correct order on page 77.

© McGraw-Hill Children's Publishing

LL80006 *Personal Hygiene*

Bathing Your Body–Lesson 3–Activity

Wash Me First

1. Color the part of your body that you wash first **purple**.

2. Color the part of your body that you wash second **blue**.

3. Color the part of your body that you wash third **green**.

4. Color the part of your body that you wash fourth **yellow**.

5. Color the part of your body that you wash fifth **orange**.

6. Color the part of your body that you wash last **red**.

Lesson 1

Using Deodorant

Objective: Student will understand the importance of using deodorant and applying it properly.

Explanation: Often students do not understand the need for deodorant and therefore do not use it. Also they may not understand when and how to apply it effectively.

Materials Needed:
- Several types and fragrances of deodorant, one per student
- Plastic doll for each student
- Paintbrush and watercolor paint for each student
- Paper towels

Directions to Teacher:

1.) Remind the students of the discussions about bacteria or little bugs, how bacteria prefers to live in warm, dark places, and that those areas can start to smell bad.

2.) Explain to the students that one of the smelliest places on the body is the underarm or armpit. Emphasize, in a funny way, what a nice place the underarms are for bacteria/bugs to live and how much the bugs love to "stink up the place."

3.) Show the students the containers of deodorant. Explain to the students that deodorant stops the bugs from growing and makes the underarms a very unpleasant place for them to live. Also let the students know that the deodorant only lasts one day (or less if they sweat a lot and wash it off), so it must be applied at least once a day and sometimes twice a day. Tell them to apply it always in the morning and after bathing.

4.) Also explain to the students that the entire underarm must be covered with deodorant.

5.) Demonstrate with a doll and watercolor paint how and where to apply the deodorant, making sure the entire area of the underarm is covered, not other areas.

6.) Allow each student to practice applying the paint to a doll's underarms in the way that deodorant should be applied. Be sure to wash off the paint before applying a new coat.

7.) When a student can complete this step correctly with paint several times, encourage him/her to choose a type of deodorant and practice applying it to the doll's underarms. Be sure to demonstrate to the students how to apply deodorant from various types of containers.

8.) Allow each student who masters this skill to keep the selected deodorant container for personal use.

Using Deodorant—Activity Sheet 1

Phew! I Stink!

Draw a circle around each picture showing when to use deodorant.

Using Deodorant—Activity Sheet 2

It's the Pits!

Color the picture to show exactly where to apply deodorant.

Lesson 1

Washing Your Hair

Objective: Student will understand the importance of washing his/her hair.

Explanation: Often, students simply do not understand that hair gets dirty and smelly. This activity will help students learn the importance of washing their hair.

Materials Needed:
- New string mop
- Oil or grease and dirty water
- Tempera paint
- Bucket of clean water or access to sink
- Liquid detergent
- Permanent fine-tipped black marker

Directions to Teacher:

1.) Show the students the new mop. Let them observe how clean it smells.

2.) Rub the mop with oil or grease, tempera paint, and lots of dirty water. Now allow the students to examine and smell the mop again. Ask them if they would like to use the dirty mop to clean the floor. (If possible, borrow the janitor's very dirty, smelly mop and let them examine an authentically dirty one.)

3.) Use the liquid detergent to clean the mop thoroughly and then let the students see and smell it. Be sure to demonstrate the soap, wash, and rinse cycle for the students to observe.

4.) Lead a discussion with the students by comparing the mop to their hair, the oil to the oil on their hands and skin, the paint to dirt on their hands and faces, and the dirty water to sweat. Discuss how people's hair gets dirty and smelly like the mop. Comment on how nobody wants to see or touch dirty hair.

5.) Explain to the students that just as the mop was cleaned with the detergent, their hair can be washed with shampoo so that it looks lovely and smells nice. Let them know that if they do not wash their hair it will become gross looking and bad smelling like the janitor's mop.

6.) Be sure to point out that unlike the mop, their hair differs in textures, the amount of scalp oils produced, and may need to be washed at different time spans. For example, people who sweat a lot or have a lot of oil on their skin have to wash their hair more frequently. And most people of African American ethnicity have dry hair that usually only needs to be washed weekly or biweekly. However, everybody needs to wash his/her hair regularly.

7.) As a group, allow the students individually to talk about their hair and how often they probably need to wash it. (*Note:* You may need to consult with another staff member of a different race to understand fully each student's hair washing needs.) Write on each student's hand the number of days he/she can wait between washes.

Name _____

Washing Your Hair—Lesson 1

Clean and Shiny Hair

Draw a line from the happy face to the people with clean hair. Draw a line from the sad face to the people who need to wash their hair.

Lesson 2

Washing Your Hair

Objective: Student will learn appropriate steps to wash his/her hair.

Explanation: Students often do not know what to do to make sure their hair is clean. This exercise will teach them how to wash their hair.

Materials Needed:
- Flash cards (see page 86–93)
- Several travel-size bottles of different types of shampoo and conditioner
- Plastic doll with hair, towel, and large toothed comb for each student
- Access to sink or pail of water for each student
- Vinyl tablecloths or newspaper
- A penny
- Fine-tipped watercolor marker

Directions to Teacher:

1.) Remind the students of the discussions you had about the reasons to wash hair; about the soap, wash, and rinse cycles; and about how much soap to use. It may be helpful to display the charts from these exercises.

2.) Using the flash cards (prepare by photocopying and mounting onto poster board) and a plastic doll, explain and demonstrate the steps for washing hair.

3.) Cover the desks or tables with vinyl cloths.

4.) Trace the penny in the middle of each student's hand as a reminder.

5.) Give each student a doll and a pail of water. Let him/her choose a bottle of shampoo and conditioner. Have them as a group, following your lead, wash the dolls' hair according to the steps outlined on the flash cards.

6.) Then have them practice individually washing each doll's hair. Provide lots of positive reinforcement for success. Allow each student who does this correctly to keep a bottle of shampoo and conditioner.

7.) As the students wash hair, have them sing the following song (use the tune of "London Bridge Is Falling Down"). First verse: "I know how to wash my hair, wash my hair, wash my hair. I know how to wash my hair to make me look real nice." Second verse: "First, I need to wet my hair, wet my hair, wet my hair. First, I need to wet my hair and make it very wet." Third verse: "Next, I soap and wash and rinse, . . . to get my hair so clean." Fourth verse: "Then I do that over again, . . . to make sure it is squeaky clean." Fifth verse: "Now I use conditioner, . . . and then I rinse and rinse." Sixth verse: "Then I towel my hair dry, . . . so I won't drip everywhere." Seventh verse: . . . "Last I comb it carefully, . . . to make me look real nice."

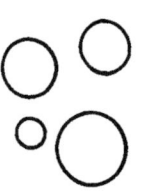

© McGraw-Hill Children's Publishing — LL80006 *Personal Hygiene*

Washing Your Hair

Lesson 2–Flash Card 1

Wet hair well.

Washing Your Hair

Lesson 2–Flash Card 2

Put about the size of a penny of shampoo in your hand. If you have long hair, you might have to use about two pennies in size.

Washing Your Hair

Lesson 2–Flash Card 3

Wash hair. Be sure to work the shampoo throughout the hair and scrub gently.

Washing Your Hair

Lesson 2–Flash Card 4

Rinse hair. Be sure to get out all of the soap.

Washing Your Hair

Lesson 2–Flash Card 5

Soap, wash, and rinse again.
Make sure to rinse well.

Washing Your Hair

Lesson 2–Flash Card 6

Put about the size of a penny of conditioner on your hand and work it into your hair. Rinse well.
If you have long hair, you may need to use about two pennies in size.

Washing Your Hair

Lesson 2–Flash Card 7

Towel dry your hair.
Be sure to dry it as much as possible.

92

© McGraw-Hill Children's Publishing

LL80006 *Personal Hygiene*

Washing Your Hair

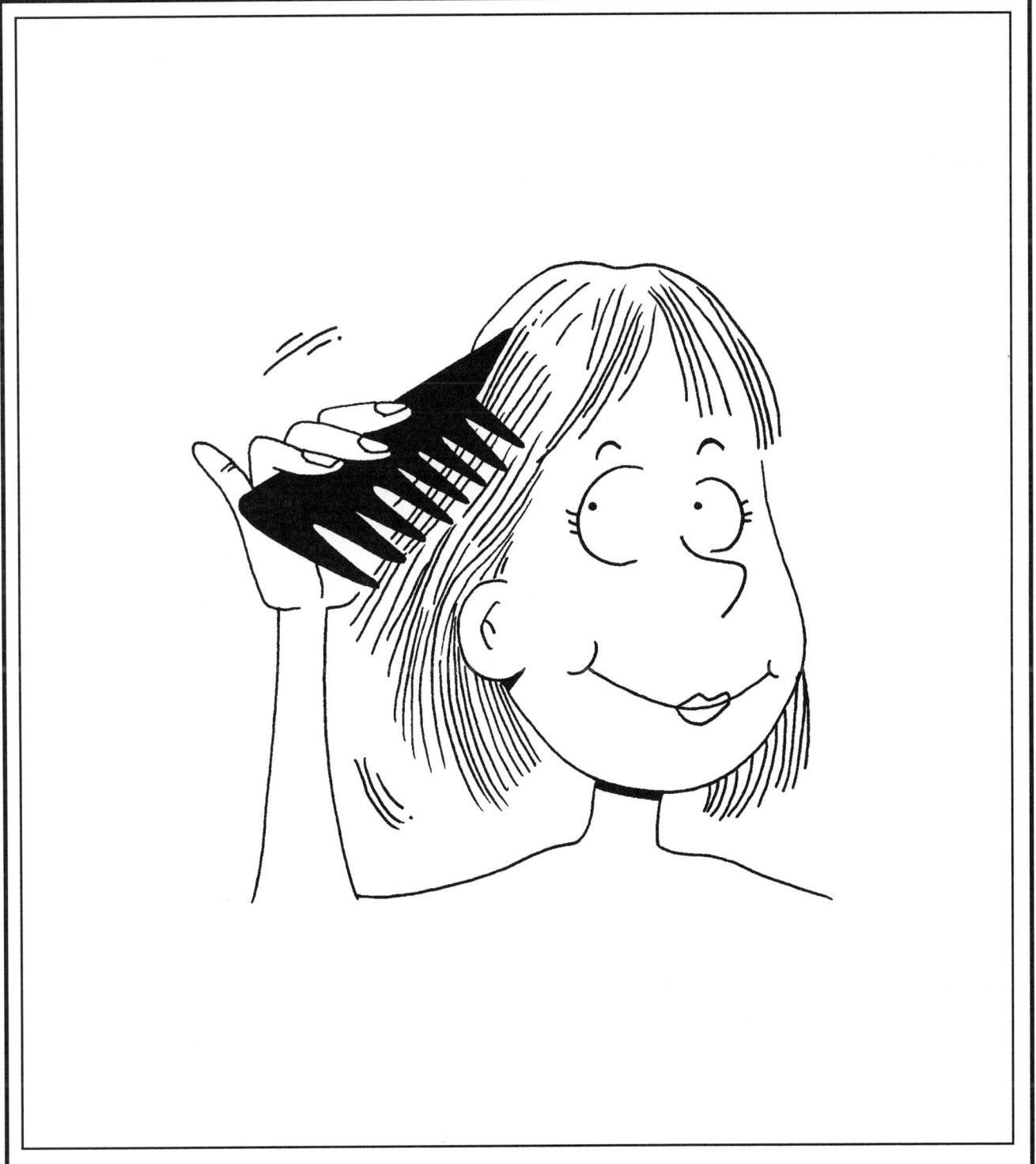

Lesson 2–Flash Card 8

Comb hair carefully. If you have tangles or your hair is long, ask for help.

Washing Your Hair–Lesson 2–Activity

Clean Hair Everywhere!

Think about the steps for washing your hair.
Paste the pictures in the correct order.

1	2
3	4
5	6
7	8

Washing Your Hair

Lesson 2–Activity

Pictures for Clean Hair Everywhere!

Cut out the pictures. Paste them in the correct order on page 94.

Personal Hygiene Award

Given to _____

Signed _____

Date _____

SOAP

© McGraw-Hill Children's Publishing

LL80006 *Personal Hygiene*